Praise for
PRAYING LIKE MONKS,
LIVING LIKE FOOLS

"Prayer is a search for help outside the self." Could any statement be more important for our time? Could any act be more essential to spiritual life in our cultural moment? This is a book for our desperate times. My friend Tyler Staton is a world-class leader, a gifted pastor, an extraordinary writer, and, above all, a man of prayer. By reading this book, you will be learning from a master.

JOHN MARK COMER, founder of Practicing the Way
and author of *The Ruthless Elimination of Hurry*

No book has ever left me wanting to pray more. In *Praying Like Monks, Living Like Fools*, Tyler Staton opens our eyes and hearts to the beauty, mystery, and value of prayer in the life of every believer and skeptic.

CHRISTINE CAINE, founder of A21 and Propel Women

To know Tyler Staton is to encounter a man who is consumed by what it means to live like Jesus. And of course it is inconceivable to live like Jesus without doing what he spent so much of his time doing, which is prayer. Tyler has both given himself to this life-giving practice and provided us with a compelling vision for prayer in the life of the Christ follower. I emerged from this book with my heart stirred to talk to God more.

DR. BRYAN LORITTS, author of *Saving the Saved*

Tyler Staton is one of America's most inspiring and gifted prayer leaders today, and his brilliant new book flows from the deepest place of his own personal life. At times it feels like holy ground. I particularly appreciated the practical exercises at the end of each chapter, as well as the closing section about the lost art of praying for the lost. Tyler serves up the full menu of prayer—from deep contemplative practices to teaching about the power and necessity of intercessory prayer. There's something here for everyone. It's both an on-ramp for those new to faith who are seeking to grow in a conversational relationship with the Lord and a master class for Christians who are seeking to be stretched and inspired. This is a vital invitation into the highest calling of every person on the planet, flowing straight from the heart of a contemporary prayer warrior, a respected pastor, and a dear friend.

PETE GREIG, founder of 24-7 Prayer International
and senior pastor of Emmaus Road Church

PRAYING LIKE MONKS, LIVING LIKE FOOLS

PRAYING LIKE MONKS, LIVING LIKE FOOLS

An Invitation to the Wonder and Mystery of Prayer

TYLER STATON

ZONDERVAN
BOOKS

ZONDERVAN BOOKS

Praying Like Monks, Living Like Fools
Copyright © 2022 by Tyler Staton

Requests for information should be addressed to:
Zondervan, *3900 Sparks Dr. SE, Grand Rapids, Michigan 49546*

Zondervan titles may be purchased in bulk for educational, business, fundraising, or sales promotional use. For information, please email SpecialMarkets@Zondervan.com.

ISBN 978-0-310-36538-9 (audio)

Library of Congress Cataloging-in-Publication Data

Names: Staton, Tyler, 1987- author.
Title: Praying like monks, living like fools : an invitation to the wonder and mystery of prayer / Tyler Staton.
Description: Grand Rapids : Zondervan, 2022. | Includes bibliographical references. | Summary: "In Praying Like Monks, Living Like Fools, Tyler Staton—author, pastor, and director of the 24-7 Prayer movement in the United States—uses biblical teaching, powerful storytelling, and historic Christian practices to offer both inspiring vision and practical instruction for how to encounter the wondrous, mysterious, living God through prayer"—Provided by publisher.
Identifiers: LCCN 2022005475 (print) | LCCN 2022005476 (ebook) | ISBN 9780310365358 (trade paperback) | ISBN 9780310365365 (ebook)
Subjects: LCSH: Prayer—Christianity. | BISAC: RELIGION / Christian Living / Spiritual Growth | RELIGION / Christian Living / Prayer
Classification: LCC BV215 .S73 2022 (print) | LCC BV215 (ebook) | DDC 248.3/2—dc23/eng /20220705
LC record available at https://lccn.loc.gov/2022005475
LC ebook record available at https://lccn.loc.gov/2022005476

Published in association with the literary agency of Wolgemuth & Associates, Inc.

Cover design: Faceout Studio / Spencer Fuller
Cover illustration: Abstractor / Shutterstock
Interior design: Sara Colley

Printed in the United States of America

23 24 25 26 27 LBC 16 15 14 13 12

For Kirsten.
You have my heart.
You always have.
You always will.

CONTENTS

FOREWORD

When I first met Tyler Staton, I was coming out of a multi-year season of a spiritual and emotional drought. I'm a Bible nerd by profession, so I never lost my love and fascination for Scripture, its literary brilliance, or its vibrant tapestry of theological themes. Jesus of Nazareth remained as compelling and beautiful to me as ever. But due to many factors I'm still sorting out, all of those things, and even Jesus himself, became more a set of ideas for me and less a dynamic person to whom I relate in my day-to-day activities. I found myself intellectually compelled by the story of Jesus, even personally moved. But I had lost touch with a way of life marked by personal connection or intimacy with the one Jesus called "Father," and therefore with Jesus himself.

What I needed was not just a new set of "techniques" to revitalize my prayer life. I didn't really know what I needed. All I knew was that Jesus felt like an artifact, and the presence of God was *an idea*, but not *an experience*. I didn't know what to do, except hope that one day something would change.

And by God's mercy, something did change. I don't know why or how exactly it happened. I had started a habit of beginning each day with a period of silence, asking God to speak to me or interact with me in a way I could hear and understand. I just needed to know there was *someone* on the other end of this conversation. To be honest, I did that for a long time without feeling anything at all.

Then, in a series of events, some very surprising things happened in my family's life. If I could let my skeptical, intellectual guard down for a moment, I genuinely felt like *someone* had not just heard my prayers but was responding to them. I was having an experience of God's presence in my life that felt real, dynamic, and unpredictable. And it was wonderful.

Having met Tyler just a few months into this experience, I saw many reasons why it would be easy to form a friendship. We both share a calling as pastors. We both really, *really* love Scripture. And we're both raising little boys. But those weren't the things our early friendship was built on. I found in Tyler someone who didn't just understand these new experiences of God's presence that I was having. He had been having these kinds of experiences with God since he was a boy. It became more and more clear that *prayer* was just one way of describing the mystery and wonder of a human living in dynamic communion with God. I found in Tyler a friend with whom I could process and question and celebrate this rediscovery of God's presence in my life.

Tyler shared with me a number of habits that he learned from others, practices that keep our minds, hearts, and bodies open to the presence and power of God's Spirit. It turns out they're quite ancient and deeply intuitive. While I knew about most of them, I had never actually tried them before, at least not in a consistent way. Then one day, Tyler told me he was bringing all of these experiences, learnings, and practices of prayer together into a book. He invited me to offer feedback on an early version, and as I did, it was like reliving all those conversations again.

In this book, Tyler provides a series of meditations on the core practices of prayer that are woven together with deep scriptural wisdom. But this isn't a book full of *ideas* about prayer. Every chapter is framed by a story from Tyler's life where he *experienced* the thing he's describing. And lest you be simply informed by new facts or entertained by a story, he ends each chapter with an invitation to do something in response—to try some new habits, practices that can create space in your life for your own experience of God's presence. But do know that because communion with God is truly relational, it's not predictable or formulaic. So you may have a different experience of this book than I did, and your own (re) discovery of God's presence will need to happen in some other way. But I'm convinced you'll benefit from Tyler's story, his scriptural reflections, and his discoveries on his journey of relating to God.

My hope is that you will come to experience prayer and the presence of God in the way Thomas Keating describes it:

> This Presence is so immense, yet so humble; awe-inspiring, yet so gentle; limitless, yet so intimate, tender and personal. I *know* that I am *known*. Everything in my life is transparent in this Presence. It knows everything about me—all my weaknesses, brokenness, sinfulness—and still loves me infinitely. This Presence is healing, strengthening, refreshing—just by its Presence . . . It is like coming home to a place I should never have left, to an awareness that was somehow always there, but which I did not recognize.[1]

Knowing this kind of loving presence, hovering in every moment of our lives, is its own category of experience. In fact, it's not "an experience" at all. It's a way of existing, of living each moment in the awareness that one's whole life is permeated with the presence of God. I'm a long way from being actively aware of that presence all day long and allowing it to transform all of my thinking and behavior. But I'm on the journey, and so is Tyler. And we hope this book can help you along that journey too.

TIM MACKIE, cofounder of the BibleProject,
Portland, Oregon

AUTHOR NOTE

Personal names in this book have been changed. While all the stories are real, I've changed people's names and other identifying details in order to protect the individuals' privacy.

Story is the precious gift that thrusts spirituality from the theoretical and into the grit and honesty of the everyday world. To be entrusted with the still-unfolding stories of so many is the greatest and most sacred of pastoral privileges.

To those who have danced, wept, wrestled, whispered, screamed, laughed, and listened in prayer alongside me—your stories are the real gift of this book. I am deeply grateful to each of you and hope I have honored you in the pages that follow.

INTRODUCTION

It's eerily quiet tonight in the city that never sleeps. The sirens and car horns, street noise from passersby, crowded restaurants and rambunctious bars—the soundtrack humming beneath the life I've known for, well, going on twelve years now—it's all gone silent. You could hear a pin drop in New York City.

I am writing to you from the modest kitchen table of my cozy Brooklyn apartment. The year is 2020, and the COVID-19 pandemic has caused unprecedented suffering, a startling interruption to "normal life," and a profound loss of security and control. Loss of control comes in an endless variety of forms—a car accident, a phone call, a financial hole we can't climb out of, a relationship we're unable to repair, or a global pandemic. Whatever its origin, it all leads to the same place: a search for help outside of the self.

How am I going to get through this? Why is this happening? What could possibly change the narrative? For many, those sorts of questions, brought on by outside events, produced an internal response: *prayer.*

Of course, for every person desperately turning to prayer in 2020, there was someone looking at the same widespread crisis and saying good riddance to God. On one side of the coin, the coronavirus pandemic is an event causing many comfortable agnostics to turn to prayer. On the other side of that very coin, though, the praying voices of many faithful churchgoers have gone silent.

The same set of circumstances that has the world turning *to* God has the church turning *from* God. The world knocks on the doors of the church, but those in the pews are scrambling for the exits. For each one desperately whispering, "Help," to God in the past year, there was another dejectedly whispering, "You're no help at all."

Both people, experiencing the same circumstances, talking to the same God. Both are forms of prayer. Both, in fact, are biblical prayers.

The Phenomenon of Prayer

Already today, before you read these words, plenty of people have prayed. Catholics have recited the poetic prayers of the historic saints. Muslims have spread out their rugs, bowed their foreheads to the ground, and begun chanting the Qur'an in unison. Jews have written pleas to Yahweh on small pieces of paper, rolled them up, and wedged them into Jerusalem's Wailing Wall. Buddhists have meditatively emptied themselves, searching for an enlightened state of self-forgetfulness. Tibetan monks have spun a wheel that holds the wadded-up pages of prayer journals, like a game of divine roulette. And somewhere, a staunch, convinced atheist in a hospital waiting room has buried his head in his hands and muttered a few desperate words to a God he doesn't even believe is there to listen. And all that was today, before you read these words.

If you are a churchgoing Christian in the West, you've become a sociological anomaly. The Western church is declining in essentially every statistical measure. Still, in a society losing interest in and growing suspicious of the church, prayer isn't going anywhere. According to reliable Gallup research, more Americans will pray in a given week than will exercise, drive a car, have sex, or go to work.[1] In an increasing post-Christian America, nearly half the population still admits praying daily, a number that dwarfs the nation's church attendance.[2] Any way you measure it, prayer is bigger than the church (and it's not close).

Everybody prays. Everybody always has. And there's no end in sight.

Prayer seems to be instinctive, a part of human nature. Primitive peoples and enlightened Westerners, rural homesteaders and urban-dwelling professionals, stay-at-home moms and touring musicians, insecure artists and ruthless investors, doubting atheists and devout creationists—they're all praying. In the words of Rabbi Abraham Joshua Heschel, "Prayer is *our* humble *answer* to the inconceivable surprise of living."[3] We pray. We can't help it.

Prayer invites you to learn to listen to God before speaking, to ask like a child in your old age, to scream your questions in an angry tirade, to undress yourself in vulnerable confession, and to be loved—completely and totally loved, in spite of everything.

And yet most people, even most Bible-believing Christians, find little life in prayer. Prayer is boring or obligatory or confusing or, most often, all of the above.

The Mystery in the Middle

Stories are often told of dramatic answers to prayer—stories that begin with desperate need and end with miraculous intervention. I'm not too interested in the beginning or even the end of the story when it comes to prayer though. What I'm interested in is the middle. The middle is where the mystery lies. The middle is where all our questions about prayer are littered.

Is prayer really necessary? If God is all-powerful, that means he accomplishes what he wants, when he wants, right? So why does he need me to ask?

Why does God sometimes seem to answer prayers, but only after a long, long period of asking? If the answer was yes, why did he make me sweat it out?

Why doesn't God answer my prayers for lost friends and family? I mean, he wants to redeem the world, right? He wants a relationship with every person. He wants to answer prayer. So if every box is checked, why isn't it happening?

I know we have a spiritual enemy. But if Jesus was victorious over Satan, then is there any real opposition left to interfere with my prayers?

What is actually happening when I pray? Is anything happening because I prayed that was not going to happen if I didn't? Or is anything not happening because I prayed that was bound to happen otherwise?

Do my prayers actually matter? Do they matter to God, and do they matter in real life in the real world? At the end of the day, what is happening in the middle?

This book is about precisely that—the mystery in the middle of our prayers.

Saints, Sleepwalkers, and Skeptics

I'm writing on prayer because prayer is the dangerous pilgrimage I'm on. And like a walk on the Camino de Santiago, it's as arduous as advertised and even more worth it than anticipated.

I'm writing on prayer because I love the church. I believe the Christian church is the hope of the world. I also love the generations who are shrugging off the church not because of spiritual disinterest but because they're taking the sincerity of their spiritual search elsewhere.

I'm writing on prayer because I trust God to be God. I

believe—really believe—that those who seek him will surely find him.[4] I believe that God is loving enough that a conversation starter is all he needs to draw someone all the way home.

I'm writing to saints, sleepwalkers, and skeptics.

To the saints, this book is an invitation into the deep end of the pool. These pages hold a collection of treasures from various eras and expressions in the Christian tradition—from the great cloud of biblical witnesses, to desert mothers and fathers, to Benedictine and Eastern Orthodox monks, to Catholic philosophers, fiery reformers, and modern evangelicals. Most of us get about knee-deep in the Christian life, discover that the water feels fine, and stop there. We never swim in the depths of the divine intimacy Jesus won for us. This book is an invitation to swim.

To the sleepwalkers, this book is a bucket of cold water doused over your drowsy head. Far too many of us find God admirable but boring. The spiritual life is the "right" way, the "good" way, but excitement is found in our social calendars, favorite sports teams, sexual conquests, or career trajectories. There is a tragic disconnect between the sacred and the secular in today's Christianity that has led to an unbiblical divorce between a "spiritual life" (made up of activities like Scripture reading, prayer, and—if you're going for extra credit—tithing) and a "normal life" (made up of basically everything else).

To the skeptics, this book is an invitation to what cannot be taught, only discovered. It's written as an open invitation to get off the comfortable fence of ultimate uncertainty and find out if God really is knowable or not. An invitation to be found by God in the place he's most faithfully been found throughout history: not in a megachurch with Broadway lights and arena-rock fog machines or in the eloquent podcast of a contrarian thinker, but in the bare silence of you and the endless expanse beyond you. "Is there an infinitely loving, altogether good Author behind this grand story or not? And if there is, what are the chances he's gently trying to catch my attention?" The answers to those questions can only be discovered. This book is an invitation to discovery through prayer.

Prayer is the intersection between an out-of-touch Western church and a spiritually curious Western world. In an increasingly post-Christian America—spiritually interested but religiously suspicious, thirsty for mystical experience but "spare me the advice of anyone deemed a 'professional,' thank you very much"—prayer is the one aspect of the historic, orthodox Christian faith that isn't threatening to the emerging sociocultural climate surrounding the church. In fact, it's inviting.

Prayer is also the theme of my life. It has been up to this point, and it will be for however many days I get to live in this occasionally beautiful, often dark world. Prayer is how I discovered God. Prayer is why I became a pastor. Prayer is the source of my life's greatest celebrations, most heartrending disappointments, and most confusing (and still unanswered) questions. Prayer is not a soft place to lay our heads or a workout routine for burning spiritual fat. It's a wild, unpredictable adventure that only those brave enough to strip themselves of artificial identities, get the wind completely knocked out of them a time or two, and see beauty in mystery will ever take. Proceed with caution. Prayer is not for the faint of heart.

Praying Like Monks, Living Like Fools is a catalog of prayer, each chapter ending with an invitation to practice—a simple starting place for moving past consideration to discovery. Don't read this book for its content; read its content for its practices. The real treasures are found after you close the book and begin the conversation.

That's where we're headed, but this story begins in a very ordinary place: the parking lot of a public middle school.

Chapter 1

HOLY GROUND

Pray As You Can

Not another soul in sight. No one else would be here at sunrise on a holiday. I sat motionless behind the wheel of a borrowed car idling in the parking lot, sobbing—overwhelmed by tears of gratitude.

I hadn't laid eyes on this building in nearly two decades, but here I was—staring at the public middle school that somehow became a temple to me, a cathedral, a meeting place, the hinge point of my whole life.

It's always the common places that turn out to be holy, isn't it? A burning bush in that same familiar field where Moses punched the clock every day for forty years. The sitting room where Esther presented her request to the king. The upstairs windowsill where Daniel rested his elbows while he defiantly prayed against royal law. The depressed old barn of a poor farmer on the outskirts of Bethlehem. The beach that Peter had docked at since he was a boy. The duplex on a seedy street in Jerusalem where the wind started blowing inside.

It only takes a moment to turn an everyday place into holy ground. That's what happened to me here.

An Experiment in Transcendence

When I was thirteen years old, I wasn't sure I was buying all the Jesus stuff. I was a curious kid, but I wasn't an easy sell. *Look, if this story is real, I want in. But if it's a fairy tale, I'd prefer to find out sooner than later so I don't waste so much time singing mediocre songs and sitting through all these meetings.* That was my logic.

Naturally, when a mentor approached me with an experiment of sorts, it caught my attention.

"What do you think God would do in the lives of your unbelieving friends if you spent every day this summer walking a circle around your school in prayer for them?"

"I have no idea."

"Why don't you find out?"

I liked that idea.

My older brother had just turned sixteen, meaning any reason to drive anywhere was a good one. Every single day that summer, he drove me to the one place I planned to avoid: school. I wore a dirt path into the thick summer grass walking the school grounds with a folded-up student directory in my right hand. This was back in the day when they gave everyone in the school everyone else's phone number. What were they thinking? Never once did I use the school directory until that summer, when it became my personal "book of common prayer," guiding the whispered words of my uncertain, pubescent voice while I paced around the outside of that familiar building, holding every last name in my soon-to-be eighth-grade class before the God I only half believed in.

Something happened to me that summer.

I fell in love with the God I wasn't sure was listening. I discovered that I didn't just "need" God in some ultimate sense; I liked

God. I enjoyed his presence. I looked forward to his company. That's all I knew for sure.

On the first day back to school, I asked to speak to the principal. I walked into the office I'd narrowly avoided the previous two years and came right out with it. I just asked him, "Can I start a new extracurricular school program—one about Jesus?"

"Well, you'll need a teacher to sponsor it. Every school club has to have a teacher sponsor. Find a teacher, and you're free to go for it."

That's how I ended up leading a Christian outreach meeting in a fluorescent-lit, white-tiled math classroom at Brentwood Middle School. We met at 6:30 a.m. on Wednesday mornings, an obviously convenient time. What twelve- or thirteen-year-old *doesn't* want to explore existential questions of origin and purpose before the sun comes up?

My entire strategy for hosting these meetings was simple. I'd sit in my bedroom on Tuesday evenings, open the Bible at random to a page somewhere in the middle, pick a paragraph on that page, read it with absolutely no other context or hint of biblical literacy, jot a few thoughts of my own interpretation on a sheet of loose-leaf paper, and then read and explain that passage to whomever showed up the following Wednesday morning. It was a recipe for disaster, not revival.

But I had one thing going for me. I prayed.

I went to school an hour early on Wednesdays to lead that group, so I went to school an hour early on Tuesdays and Thursdays to keep thumbing through that now pocket-creased, heavily frayed, and worn-out school directory, praying name by name for my classmates. My mom, the believer who led me to faith, actually sat me down and asked me to chill out with all the prayer because she was losing too much sleep taking me to school so early—true story.

A couple months into these meetings, so many students were

coming that we had to move from a math classroom into the school's theater. By the end of that school year, approximately one-third of my eighth-grade class had come into relationship with Jesus in the darkness of the early morning, with all the atmosphere of hospital lighting, through the potentially heretical sermons of a thirteen-year-old skeptic.

It's either completely ludicrous or utterly breathtaking to think that in the midst of all the insecurity of a thirteen-year-old boy—the nervousness of going out for the basketball team, the awkward (and slightly late) arrival of puberty, the sweaty palms of school dances—there was also the Spirit of the living God bending history in loving response to the prayed mumblings of a kid. And not because he finds that kid particularly brilliant or his suggestions on how to run the world innovative, but simply because he finds this kid in all of his insecurity, awkwardness, and adolescent nervousness to be irresistibly lovable.

That's ludicrous, or it's breathtaking.

Take Off Your Shoes

All of that was twenty years ago now as I sat in a borrowed car in that old familiar parking lot, slowly prying open the door on the driver's side. When my foot hit the pavement, the sun was just beginning to backlight the sleepy, gray sky. There was a fanned-out line of parked yellow school buses resting for the holidays. Every door to the building was chain-locked and bolted shut, not that I had any intention of going in. It was walking around the outside that had drawn me here at this hour. I wanted to walk the ground where I'd worn the tread off my shoes in prayer laps—the little loop that had come to define my spiritual life.

I was now thirty-one, a pastor in Brooklyn, New York.

My family had moved out of this town shortly after that defining eighth-grade year, and I hadn't been back to Brentwood since. I hadn't returned to this place, but this place, what happened here, never left me.

My in-laws live about a half hour away from the school, and I was at their house for Christmas. I got to thinking, *I haven't laid eyes on that school building in twenty years.*

So I drove back there. Timed my arrival for 6:30 a.m., just for old times' sake.

"Take off your sandals, for the place where you are standing is holy ground."[1]

I slipped off my shoes and felt the ice-cold pavement cut right through my socks.

I stood in that cleft cut for a flagpole on the hill that rolled down the school's front lawn—the hidden place where I used to sit as a thirteen-year-old praying by name for my friends most Tuesdays. I walked over to that patch of sidewalk where I sat on Thursdays, alone at first, a group of adolescent revivalists gradually growing around me as that year wore on. I walked the exact path I wore into the grass as I circled that building in prayer, and as I did, the space between heaven and earth seemed paper-thin.

To everyone else, this is a dingy, old public middle school in need of government funding and mild renovations. To me, this is holy ground. This is the place where God started something in me that has never stopped. This is the place where I found out what Jesus was talking about when he said, "If you remain in me and my words remain in you, ask whatever you wish, and it will be done for you."[2] So I walked that ground and prayed, with tears streaming down my face through a trembling voice that could barely get a word out.

Pray about Everything

There are plenty of biblical passages on prayer, so there is no shortage of places to start grappling with this sacred mystery. However, it probably never gets more concise and straightforward than Paul's instructions to the church at Philippi near the end of his letter:

> The Lord is near. Do not be anxious about anything, but in every situation, by prayer and petition, with thanksgiving, present your requests to God. And the peace of God, which transcends all understanding, will guard your hearts and your minds in Christ Jesus.[3]

One of the more frustrating aspects of Scripture is that it rarely reads like Ikea instructions. If God would just lay it out, step-by-step, then I'd do it. But for some reason, he's determined to speak in stories, analogies, and riddles.

This passage is proof that it's not that simple. Right here, it's laid out step-by-step, but generally speaking, we don't follow the steps. *Do not be anxious about anything. Pray about everything.* But most Christ followers spend far more hours turning over anxious thoughts than surrendering them in prayer. If it's right there, so plain and clear, why not take God up on such a satisfying exchange?

Short answer: we don't buy it.

We think, *Come on, it's just not that simple.*

As pastor of a church primarily filled with young adults in the first half of life, I get a lot more questions about managing anxiety than I get about prayer. Anxiety is the soundtrack humming beneath modern life, so I have plenty of conversations with anxious people.

It's not just a diagnosis of others though. The truth is, *I'm* more familiar with anxiety than I am with peace. I'm better acquainted with a subconscious drive to control the circumstances overwhelming me than with accepting the unburdening freedom promised in prayer. I'm not a master counselor on the other side of the divide who is offering you the miracle mantra. I'm right there with you.

God promises peace—a supernatural sort of peace we can't even logically reason out—in place of crippling anxiety. The means of this exchange is prayer. But most people, regardless of spiritual maturity, stage of life, psychological awareness, or personality type, do not experience the "anxiety for peace" exchange promised through prayer.

So why not?

Why Don't We Pray?

The obvious obstacles to prayer live on the surface. You're busy. You're social. You're (at least trying to be) successful and desirable and socially conscious. All of those things take time, so the competition for your undivided attention is stiff.

And of course, there's the fact that you carry the internet around in your pocket: 97 percent of Americans own a cell phone, and for 85 percent of them, it's a smartphone of some kind.[4] Every down moment is now spent on Reddit threads, scrolling an Instagram feed, or getting into political arguments on Twitter. So you're busy, and you're distracted.

Still, you likely find time to eat and sleep and maybe even exercise with some consistency. Even in a very busy, very distracted world, people still make time for what really matters to them. So there's something deeper, beneath the surface, that keeps us from praying.

I think it's this: for most of us, prayer doesn't resolve our anxiety. Scripture teaches, "Don't be anxious. Just pray." Maybe we don't because prayer comes with plenty of reasons to be anxious. Prayer itself makes us anxious because it uncovers fears we can ignore as long as we don't engage deeply, thoughtfully, vulnerably with God.

First, we must name the fears.

1. We Don't Pray for Fear of Being Naive

The scenes of my life play out against the backdrop of a fiercely logical, intellectual city. In that environment, there is no greater sin than naivete. In a city like New York or Portland (I've spent my entire adult life between the two), there is nothing less fashionable than a state school grad from a Midwestern suburb fresh off the plane and wide-eyed in the big city. Innocence is terribly out of style.

Everything we interact with in this small, cramped, secular world of our own making, we have the potential of mastering. In fact, we must master it quickly in order to survive—the most efficient route between home and the office, how to move up the ranks at work, how to eat sushi without looking stupid, how to cut across lanes on our bicycles and live to tell the tale. And if we can't master it, we can always avoid it. I'll just change industries, avoid chopsticks, and take an Uber.

Prayer can't be mastered. Prayer always means submission. To pray is to willingly put ourselves in the unguarded, exposed position. There is no climb. There is no control. There is no mastery. There is only humility and hope.

To pray is to risk being naive, to risk believing, to risk playing the fool. To pray is to risk trusting someone who might let you down. To pray is to get our hopes up. And we've learned to avoid that. So we avoid prayer.

2. We Don't Pray for Fear of Silence

Many people are pretty comfortable with the spirituality they've got, and prayer—as well as living like everything Jesus says about prayer is true—risks the possibility of silence.

"Silence is frightening because it strips us as nothing else does, throwing us upon the stark realities of our life," writes Dallas Willard. "And in that quiet, what if there turns out to be very little to 'just us and God'?"[5]

What if I actually strip away the music and the community and the sermon, strip away all the noise of my familiar faith expression? Left with just me and God, what if I discover there's actually not much to just me and God?

Prayer means the risk of facing silence where we're addicted to noise. It's the risk of facing a God we've mastered talking about, singing about, reading about, and learning about. It means risking real interaction with that God, and the longer we've gotten used to settling for the noise around God, the higher the stakes. What if it's awkward or disappointing or boring, or what if God stands me up altogether?

When we've got that much to lose, prayer might be scarier than the avoidance of never being alone with God.

3. We Don't Pray for Fear of Selfish Motives

We are paralyzed by self-evaluation. Prayer sputters when we evaluate and second-guess the words we speak to God as they come out of our mouths.

Why do I really want this? What's behind this request? Have I really put in enough time with God to ask for something like this, or am I just texting him when I need something? Is this desire really pure enough to bring before God?

Let's say, hypothetically, your roommate doesn't know Jesus.

Before uttering a word of prayer for her, you're confronted by a question that spirals inward. Why *really* do I want my roommate to find God? Is it because of a pure desire for her to be met by divine love that makes her whole? Or do I find comfort in someone else reaching the same conclusion I've made, like if this whole thing is just a superstitious way of making life bearable, at least they'll laugh at *us* one day, not just *me*?

Or do I think I've got all the answers and the world would be better if everyone thought like me, believed like me, and behaved like me? Am I just cloaking narcissism in faux compassion? Or is it that I carry around some sort of religious guilt my conservative grandma drilled into me as a kid, so now I pray for my roommate but it's really just to feel okay about myself?

We know all too well the cacophony of motives forever swirling inside us. When we pray, we become increasingly aware of those motives. And some are paralyzed by the subsequent self-evaluation.

4. We Don't Pray for Fear of Doing It Wrong

Some of us are kept from praying because we listen to everyone else's prayers and it makes us feel like we're next up after Winston Churchill in high school speech class.

I'm not eloquent. I'm not confident. I'm not comfortable. I hear other people pray out loud, and it only furthers the insecurity.

Many Christians spend years limiting their experience of prayer to sitting in a pew while a professional Christian talks to God in words they'd never use in normal conversation, leading to the misconception, "I must be doing it wrong."

Some of us don't pray often, not yet anyway. Maybe one day we'll master the lingo and learn the mechanics.

Why Pray?

There we have the fears, and if all that's true, then why *would* we pray?

1. Pray Because You're Overwhelmed

The great social sin of the modern world is naivete. Belief is out; cynicism is in. Where did that modern phenomenon come from?

Historically, the Enlightenment set forth the great myth of human progress, which assumes that with the passing of time, everything is improving, people are becoming more whole, and the world is getting steadily better. That assumption, which served as the backbone of the developing world, was deflated by two world wars and the bloodiest, most barbaric century in recorded history. The balloon was popped on the optimism of human progress, leading to an equally widespread sweep of disillusionment.

You and I have been groomed by a post-Enlightenment story of deconstruction that doesn't trust God anymore but has plenty of reasons not to trust people either. The result is multiple generations of people who find safety in pretending they don't need either one—I can trust myself, guide myself, be enough for myself.

Jesus once wisely said that we'll know a tree by its fruit.[6] So what's the fruit of that story of self-sufficiency in the life of the modern person? We're overwhelmed. Everyone I meet is drowning in "their thing." It doesn't matter if "your thing" is an artistic endeavor, profit margins, wining and dining clients, or raising children. We can't see past "our thing" because "our thing" (whatever it happens to be) is all-consuming.

We've avoided becoming naive, but we've done it at the cost of becoming overwhelmed. The story that was supposed to free us is really just swapping jail cells. If the story we thought would free us is trapping us, the logical thing to do is look beyond it. Instead, even in the church, our prayers don't exchange overwhelmed lives for transcendent peace. They simply drag God into our overwhelmed lives, and the only way we can make him fit is to shrink him down to a reduced size. We keep on praying, but we lower the bar of expectation and power in prayer.

We kick like mad to keep our heads above water, all the while talking passively to an imagined God who is powerless to do most anything except give us the right perspective to make it through the day. We dwindle God down to a divine Being just as overwhelmed and powerless as we are, and our prayers to that God are understandably vague and infrequent.

Constantly overwhelmed lives should drive us to prayer at its purest and rawest, but the tendency for many of us is to pray safe, calculated prayers that insulate us from both disappointment and freedom.

2. Pray Because Trust Comes before Faith

We fear silence. But the thing that calms that fear isn't faith; it's trust. Faith is the assurance of what we hope for.[7] Trust is confidence in the character of God.

Before we can have faith that God will answer a given request, we simply have to learn to trust the character of the God we're talking to. In my experience, trying to will faith into the equation doesn't make the possibility of silence any less terrifying, but trusting the character of the listener certainly does. Trust allows us to say, "I don't understand what God is doing right now, but I trust that God is good."

What if I pray and the cancer doesn't disappear? Or I don't get the job? Or she doesn't come back? Or he's still addicted?

Without trust, we suppress the disappointment that God's silence leaves with us. We build a wall to protect ourselves from the very God we pray to. We carefully nuance our prayers, guarding ourselves against allowing God to disappoint us like that a second time (we'll get deep into the weeds of unanswered prayer in chapter 9).

With trust, we can come to the God whose character doesn't seem to match his silence, saying with brutal honesty, "Where were you? How could you? What were you thinking?"

Jesus hasn't revealed a God we can perfectly understand, but he has revealed a God we can perfectly trust. Trust is the certainty that the listening God hears and cares. I trust the God who, even when he doesn't make the suffering go away, wears the suffering alongside me. Trusting the God revealed in Jesus means silence is real, but it's not forever.

3. Pray Because Complaints Are Welcome

God isn't nearly as worried about our mixed motives as we are. I can prove it. Here's a few prayers that made the cut as part of the inspired, inerrant, canonical Scriptures:

> May burning coals fall on them;
>> may they be thrown into the fire,
>> into miry pits, never to rise. (Psalm 140:10)

> I am worn out calling for help;
>> my throat is parched.
> My eyes fail,
>> looking for my God. (Psalm 69:3)

> I pour out before him my complaint;
>> before him I tell my trouble. (Psalm 142:2)

Anger, depression, complaint. Whoever wrote those needs to see a professional.

David—that's who wrote those prayers. You've probably heard of David—ancient Israel's most famous figure, the king who set an unreachable bar for all subsequent kings, the man after God's own heart, the one whose bloodline was promised to lead to the Messiah. He's the psychotic nightmare who wrote those prayers. They were collected into the Psalms, which have framed Christian worship and prayer since before the church's inception.[8] Those prayers sit right alongside some of David's more revered poetry.

> The LORD is my shepherd, I lack nothing.
>> He makes me lie down in green pastures,
> he leads me beside quiet waters,
>> he refreshes my soul. (Psalm 23:1–3)

Well, apparently David wasn't always that serene and balanced because he also prayed, "May burning coals fall on them."[9]

> Praise the LORD, my soul,
>> and forget not all of his benefits . . .
> who satisfies your desires with good things
>> so that your youth is renewed like the eagle's.
>>> (Psalm 103:2, 5)

He mustn't always have felt like God was spreading his wings because he also prayed, "I am worn out calling for help."[10]

> Every day I will praise you
>> and extol your name for ever and ever.
>>> (Psalm 145:2)

I guess that "every day" was hyperbolic because some days it wasn't praise on his lips: "I pour out before him my complaint."[11]

The psalms reveal a garden variety of motives. Some of the words in those prayers go directly against the teachings of Jesus and the character of God (What happened to loving enemies and a God who is rich in love and loyal in faithfulness?[12]), meaning some of the psalms are technically heretical. So why would those prayers be included in the Bible?

Because they're honest. That's what makes these psalms exemplary. God is looking for relationship, not well-prepared speeches spoken from perfect motives. God listened to overreacting rage, dramatic despair, and guileless joy, and he called David a man after his own heart.[13] When it comes to prayer, God isn't grading essays; he's talking to children. So if God can delight in prayers as dysfunctional as the ones we find wedged into the middle of the Bible, he can handle yours too without you cleaning them up first.

If the Bible tells us anything about how to pray, it says that God much prefers the rough draft full of rants and typos to the polished, edited version. C. S. Lewis said of prayer, "We must lay before Him what is in us, not what ought to be in us."[14]

The way your motives change isn't by working them out in silence; it's through such brutal honesty with God that he, by prayer, can refine your motives. Complaints are welcome.

4. Pray Because the Only Way to Get It Wrong Is by Trying to Get It Right

I find it so helpful that when teaching his disciples to pray, Jesus included this line right in the middle: "Give us today our daily bread."[15]

What a simple request! Bring your felt needs to God—the needs of this day—and talk to him about them. How should we pray? The most straightforward response is to talk to God about what's on your mind. That's it! You talk to God like a friend. You vent. You ask. You laugh. You listen. You unload. You just talk.

You don't try to sound more holy or pure or spiritual than you are. Prayer isn't a noble monologue; it's a free-flowing conversation, and the only way to get prayer wrong is to try to get it right.

In the wise words of Candler School of Theology professor emerita Roberta Bondi, "If you are praying, you are already 'doing it right.'"[16]

The Lord Is Near

The Lord is near. Do not be anxious about anything, but in every situation, by prayer and petition, with thanksgiving, present your requests to God. And the peace of God, which transcends all understanding, will guard your hearts and your minds in Christ Jesus.

Philippians 4:5–7

To our modern ears, that reads like it was written by someone who's never really been anxious, someone who's never been through what I've been through. That sounds like religious well-wishing. It's just not that simple. If it's that simple, why isn't it working?

Most often, when this famous passage is referenced, it starts with the command to rid oneself of anxiety: "Do not be anxious about anything." But the passage doesn't start there. Preceding the imperative is a statement of fact: "The Lord is near."

The deep fear that robs our prayers of power is the lie that the Lord *isn't* near. The lie that God has forgotten me, that I'm not in good hands, that my future isn't secure. It's the worry that, at the end of the day, this God, near or far, can't be trusted, that he's something less than who he promises to be, and that—really, when it comes right down to it—I'm on my own.

All four gospel authors remember Jesus flipping over the

tables of the temple's money changers in a holy tantrum. He prophetically scrubbed the sacred temple clean of the corruption staining the house of prayer. And in the midst of that rampage, with every eye on the rabbi-gone-mad, Jesus yelled through panted breaths, "Stop turning my Father's house into a market!"[17] It wasn't in a composed, well-prepared moment of teaching but in the throes of righteous anger—speaking from the gut, not the head—that Jesus instinctively called the temple "my Father's house."

That's significant because in first-century Israel, the temple was the most revered building on earth. The Jewish people believed it was literally the house of Yahweh—the place where God's presence dwelt. The house God lived in. There were cleansing rituals required just to cross the threshold, and restricted access the nearer you got to the center. Even most priests couldn't enter the innermost room because in ancient Hebrew spirituality, the temple *was* the presence of God. And Jesus is calling that very place "home." In the presence of a God who made even the priests tense up, Jesus was at home.

Nancy Mairs profoundly observed, "Who one believes God to be is most accurately revealed not in any credo but in the way one speaks to God when no one else is listening."[18]

When you utter the words "Dear God," what's the expression on the divine face you're exchanging glances with? What's going through God's mind? What's God's mood?

Dear God, sorry to bother you . . .

Dear God, I know you're really busy, but . . .

Dear God, I know I haven't stopped by in a while . . .

"My Father's house." That's a profoundly different starting place from which Jesus' prayers emerge. The one, simple assurance that fills our prayers with power is "the Lord is near."

"The most important discovery you will ever make is the love the Father has for you," writes Pete Greig, founder of the 24-7 Prayer Movement. "Your power in prayer will flow from the certainty that the One who made you likes you, he is not scowling at you, he is on your side . . . Unless our mission and our acts of mercy, our intercession, petition, confession, and spiritual warfare begin and end in the knowledge of the Father's love, we will act and pray out of desperation, determination, and duty instead of revelation, expectation, and joy."[19]

The most important discovery you will ever make is the Father's love, and it's just that—a discovery. It cannot be taught. It has to be discovered, and everything else flows from that discovery.

I know that the moon is more than two hundred thousand miles away from the earth and that it's more than a light in the night sky; it's a solid mass you can touch and walk on.[20] I know that, but Neil Armstrong has discovered it. He traveled all those miles and walked on that glowing night-light. That's a different experience entirely. Knowledge is hearsay. It's memorizing the facts. Discovery requires personal experience.

You can read the description of every entrée on the menu, listen to the server's eloquent description of the few that draw your attention, and carefully watch the plates coming out, eyeing the reactions of restaurant patrons as they take the first bite. But none of it will satisfy your hunger. Until you pick up a fork and knife and taste for yourself, it's all just hearsay.

You can watch every rom-com ever produced. Read all the classic romance novels. Eavesdrop on the first date at the café table next to you. You can tear up at wedding ceremonies and admire the old couple celebrating their fiftieth anniversary, but all of that is merely to know about love. To discover love, you must feel the first-date butterflies for yourself, tell the other person how you feel with no guaranteed reciprocation, make vows in front of friends and family, and hold the wrinkled hand of your elderly spouse after decades of living out those vows through ordinary days and unexpected changes. True love requires personal experience.

When it comes to prayer, you can read all the classics, study the revival stories, and treasure up every biblical insight. You can memorize the facts. Or you can live daily in relationship with God through prayer, insist on processing the extraordinary, the devastating, and all the mundanity in the middle with the eagerly listening Father. Guess which method is more effective? Prayer is learned by discovery.

More Practice Than Theory

Jesus was asked by his disciples, "Teach us to pray."[21] And he started praying. That was his answer.

The modern father of spiritual discipline, Richard Foster, counsels, "By praying we learn to pray."[22] The contemplative Thomas Merton wrote, "If you want a life of prayer, the way to get it is by praying."[23] The spiritual giant Mother Teresa instructed, "If we really mean to pray and want to pray we must be ready to do it now."[24]

Prayer is more practice than theory, so let me offer a starting place, with a phrase borrowed from Dom John Chapman: "Pray as you can, and don't try to pray as you can't."[25] If you can't pray for an hour, great. Don't try. It'll feel like an eternity. Pray for a minute. "Pray as you can, and don't try to pray as you can't."

If you zone out every time you try to pray at home, pray while you're running errands or exercising or walking down the sidewalk.

If you can't concentrate enough to pray aloud, journal prayers with paper and pen.

If you can't pray with hope and faith, God isn't bothered. He wants you to tell him about your doubt and disappointment.

If you can't pray in phrases of praise and adoration, don't fake it. Pray your complaints, your anger, or your confusion.

And if you're more comfortable with cynicism than innocence, unsure about your motives, afraid of silence, afraid of an answer, or pretty confident you aren't doing it right, you're in the perfect starting place.

Pray as you *can*, and somewhere along the way, you will make the most important discovery of your life—the love the Father has for you. That discovery is God's end of the deal. Your part is just to show up honestly. Show up, and keep showing up. That's the one nonnegotiable when it comes to prayer.

And that invitation is for everybody.

If you've never uttered a word of prayer, you should know that one humble request was enough for a career thief crucified next to Jesus to discover the Father's love.[26]

If prayer is the source of a deep wound or disappointment for you, remember that when trust is broken in a relationship, it doesn't get healed by silence and distance; healing requires the courage of re-engaging. I won't pretend that's easy. But it is the place of healing.

If you're years into an active life of mature prayer and beginning to wonder what's left to discover, remember that you'll spend eternity in the presence of God and never reach the end of him. You'll never lose a sense of wonder at his goodness, never grow bored in his presence, and never have him all figured out. There is discovery ad infinitum in this divine relationship.

Pray as you *can*.

That's an invitation for everybody—the rookies, the jaded, the faithful, and everyone in between.

New Year's Eve 2018

One visit back to the old middle school wasn't enough for me. I had to go back. On New Year's Eve, I went out to dinner with my wife, and after dessert, I went for it. "You know where a romantic place would be to ring in the New Year?"

I drove as fast as I could across a couple towns, back to the old middle school because I wanted to be circling it in prayer when the clock turned.

I went back, not because I thought if I did, God would do what I wanted him to do. I didn't go back because there's some kind of mystical power in lining God up with the numbers on our calendar; I went back because that's where I wanted to be. I wanted to be with the Father.

And that night, again finding my car to be the only one in the parking lot, again walking my personal holy ground in prayer, I didn't become any more his son. God didn't love me more that night than he has any other night, and I didn't belong to him any more entirely than any other person out dancing and doing champagne toasts.

But in a world that for the most part rejects him, ignores him, and chooses any distraction over him, imagine how much it must bless the heart of the Father to hear, "I want to be with you. I choose you, God, over every other option."

Prayer is about presence before it's about anything else. Prayer doesn't begin with outcomes. Prayer is the free choice to be with the Father, to prefer his company. In our desire for certain outcomes or our confusion over not getting certain outcomes, we are tempted to begin there. But we cannot brush past simply being with the Father and arrive at anything close to the sort of prayer Jesus won back for us. Prayer starts with presence.

So there I am, walking around this school, the familiar prayer circle that's defined my life, as Kirsten, mother to two little ones at the time, patiently works a breast pump in the idling car. What God started in me as a thirteen-year-old kid never stopped. Everything else in my life has changed, but this is constant: I spend the waking hours of the morning preferring the Father's presence. At thirteen, it was 6:30 a.m. at the school before the teachers even bothered showing up. At thirty-one, it was the rooftop of my Brooklyn apartment building, having acrobatically scaled a fire escape with a cup of coffee in hand to access. Now at thirty-four, it's walking a pathway through Laurelhurst Park in the heart of Portland in the dark of the early morning with a quickly cooling mug of coffee in my right hand. Why? Because in spite of everything, I still prefer God's presence to anything else. It's not the gritting your teeth, "come on God, you owe me this" kind of prayer. It's being present to the One who chose me first and chooses me again today. It's the joy of my life.

And that New Year's night in particular, as the clock was turning and so was the calendar, and I was walking a path of prayer that symbolized so much for me, I could only get one prayer out through tears of passion and a quivering voice.

"Do it again, Lord.

"What I saw you do here in this ordinary place among ordinary people, do it again. Do it again, this time in Brooklyn.

"You haven't changed, so I'll keep asking: 'Do it again, Lord.'"

PRACTICE

Pray As You Can

Start where you are. Put down this book and talk to God. Talk to him about the little details of your life you're sure he doesn't care about. Talk to him about the ways he has let you down or disappointed you. Talk to him about the blessings heaped on you that you could never deserve. Talk to him about the anxiety you're carrying today. Just talk to him. Prayer is not the memorizing of facts or highlighting of key phrases; it's a relational discovery.

I have been guided into prayer, again and again, by the poetry of Ted Loder:

Holy One,
there is something I wanted to tell you, but there have been
errands to run,
    bills to pay,
        arrangements to make,
            meetings to attend,
                friends to entertain,
                    washing to do . . .
and I forget what it is I wanted to say to you,
    and mostly I forget what I'm about
        or why.
O God,
don't forget me, please,
for the sake of Jesus Christ.

Eternal One,
there is something I wanted to tell you,
but my mind races with worrying and watching,
    with weighing and planning,
        with rutted slights and pothole grievances,
            with leaky dreams and leaky plumbing
                and leaky relationships I keep trying to plug up;
and my attention is preoccupied
    with loneliness,

with doubt,
and with things I covet;
and I forget what it is I want to say to you,
and how to say it honestly
or how to do much of anything.
O God,
don't forget me, please,
for the sake of Jesus Christ.

Almighty One,
there is something I wanted to ask you,
but I stumble along the edge of a nameless rage,
haunted by a hundred floating fears
of terrorists of all kinds,
of losing my job,
of failing,
of getting sick and old,
having loved ones die,
of dying . . .
I forget what the real question is that I wanted to ask,
and I forget to listen anyway
because you seem unreal and far away,
and I forget what it is I have forgotten.
O God,
don't forget me, please,
for the sake of Jesus Christ . . .

O Father . . . in Heaven,
perhaps you've already heard what I wanted to tell you.
What I wanted to ask is
forgive me,
heal me,

increase my courage, please.
Renew in me a little of love and faith,
and a sense of confidence,
and a vision of what it might mean
to live as though you were real,
and I mattered,
and everyone was sister and brother.

What I wanted to ask in my blundering way is
don't give up on me,
don't become too sad about me,
but laugh with me,
and try again with me,
and I will with you, too.

What I wanted to ask is
for peace enough to want and work for more,
for joy enough to share,
and for awareness that is keen enough
to sense your presence
here,
now,
there,
then,
always.[27]

Chapter 2

BE STILL AND KNOW

Prayer Posture

Be still, and know that I am God;
I will be exalted among the nations,
I will be exalted in the earth.

Psalm 46:10

So we get to step two," CJ announced, "which turns out to be all about believing in and depending on a power greater than yourself."

CJ owed his few months of sobriety mostly to an AA group he had joined. He was recounting to me a recent conversation with Owen, his sponsor.

If you're not familiar with the "Big Book" of Alcoholics Anonymous, it has a lot of "God" language in it. Most 12-step groups, for the sake of inclusivity, have adopted the language of "higher power."

"Hey, man, here's the deal," CJ explained to Owen. "I want to get sober. I'm committed to the program, but I'm out on God. Don't misunderstand me. I'm in for everything else, but please don't try to talk me into some cosmic therapist to help me say 'no thanks' to a gin and tonic."

That's a fair summary of how plenty of people feel about prayer. There's been an Eastern spiritual renaissance in the modern West of late, particularly in urban areas among the educated class of emerging generations. Practices like Buddhist mindfulness, meditative emptying, yoga (even yoga accompanied by chanting in an unknown language to an unknown god)—anything that gets anyone to some elusive "centered state"—are on the table.

So, yeah, I'll pray, many subconsciously think—if by "prayer" we're talking exclusively about something happening in me, some kind of spiritual meditation. *I can get on board with that.* But actual communication with a divine being? A divine being intelligent enough to have created me, everything I know, and everything I experience? Come on. If such a being exists, the idea that he (or she or they) would be at my beck and call for conversation is pretty absurd.

So a couple days later, Owen calls up CJ, just as the workday is drawing to a close, and says, "I'm in front of your place in my car. Come on out and get in the car."

"Where we goin'?" CJ asks.

"Just get in."

They drive deep into Brooklyn, the car finally backing into a vacant spot with an expired meter along the Coney Island boardwalk.

The two of them walk out onto the beach together on a brisk November day. They sit down on the sand next to each other and just look, watching the sun set over the horizon, the gray-blue water extending far beyond what they can see. As the cold wind whips against their faces and cuts through their jackets, they just look, neither of them speaking for a minute or two.

Eventually, Owen breaks the silence with a question: "See anything here more powerful than you are?"

CJ hesitates and then says slowly, "Yeah."

"Great," Owen said. "Start there."

Owen drove CJ where he wasn't going on his own to show him what he wasn't seeing for himself.

"See anything more powerful than you?" In other words, "Can you see yourself—your tiny self—in the midst of this vast expanse beyond you? Can you see yourself from God's perspective for just a moment?" Owen was introducing CJ to the stillness and wonder from which all prayer emerges.

Prayer doesn't begin with us; it begins with God. It doesn't start with speaking; it starts with seeing. As Philip Yancey writes, "Prayer is the act of seeing reality from God's point of view."[1]

Before we open our lips and say a single word to God, we have to discover the proper posture. But we'll need the right sponsor—a mentor in prayer who will take us where we weren't planning to go to show us what we aren't currently seeing. For that, we turn to David, who has more prayers recorded in the Bible than anyone else (by a long shot). Psalm 46 is attributed to the sons of Korah, a shorthand title for the crew David gathered for night and day prayer in the tabernacle. From that community come these famous words: "Be still, and know that I am God."[2] Prayer starts there.

Be Still

We begin with just these two words of the poetic prayer of the sons of Korah: "Be still." That seems simple enough, right? It's actually much more complicated than it sounds because the way of life you and I have grown accustomed to as normal is actually historically abnormal and makes stillness nearly impossible.

The historically abnormal but universally accepted modern, Western lifestyle is largely the result of three groundbreaking inventions: the clock, the light bulb, and the iPhone.[3]

The Clock

In 1370, the first public clock was set up in Germany. Historians popularly point to that moment as the turning point when the world shifted from natural time to artificial time. Previously, people awoke with the sun's rising and went to bed with its setting.[4] There was a rhythm to life, with longer days in the summer and shorter days in the winter (which, I assume, is how people made it through German winters before central heating—they mostly slept through it).

As of 1370, when people started managing their time artificially, time shifted from being a limit governing our lives to a resource used according to our individual agendas.

The Light Bulb

In 1879, Thomas Edison invented the light bulb, which, among other things, cut way back on our sleep time. Prior to the light bulb, the average American slept ten hours a night.[5] With the increased potential for human productivity, technology took off.

By 1960, central air conditioning and heating, microwaves, dishwashers, and laundry machines were common in American homes. Around that time, sociologists commonly started making predictions about what human life would look like by the time you and I are living in, and pretty much everyone was on the same page—a dramatic increase in leisure and ease of life.

A Senate subcommittee in 1967 jointly predicted that by 1985, the average American would work twenty-two hours a week for twenty-seven weeks a year because of all the leisure time this new technology would free up.[6] In reality, "the average time people spend on leisure has *decreased* since the 1980s."[7]

Technology has continued to advance and save us time. They got that part right. What they misjudged was how we'd use it. We've spent that time on things other than deep rest.

The iPhone

How have we used that time? Well, when Apple released the first iPhone in June 2007, they gave us a tracking device for that very data. A 2016 study found that the average iPhone user touches their phone 2,617 times a day, staring at their phone screen for two and a half hours over seventy-six sessions.[8] A more recent 2019 study discovered that in just three years, the figure had more than doubled to over five hours a day.[9]

Instead of slowing down and harnessing technology to free up leisure time, we now suffer from what mental health professionals call "hurry sickness," a behavioral pattern characterized by continual rushing and anxiety. In a society that prizes efficiency and productivity above all else, that uses time like a tool rather than a limit, hurry isn't an occasional necessity; it's the new normal. "Be still." It's not as simple as it sounds.

The Christian philosopher Dallas Willard was once asked, "What do I need to do to be spiritually healthy?" After a long pause, he offered this (now famous) response: "You must ruthlessly eliminate hurry from your life."[10] According to Willard, hurry is the great enemy of spiritual life in our day. That's interesting, isn't it? I find that interesting because if I were to ask any number of spiritual teachers—pastors, priests, rabbis, and theologians—"What is the great spiritual enemy of our day?" I doubt very many of them would instinctively respond with, "Hurry."

Michael Zigarelli of Messiah University did a five-year study of twenty thousand Christians in the United States and identified "busyness" as the number one distraction from life with God. He summarizes his own research with this great conclusion:

> It may be the case that (1) Christians are assimilating to a culture of busyness, hurry and overload, which leads to (2) God becoming more marginalized in Christians' lives, which leads to (3) a deteriorating relationship with God, which leads to (4) Christians becoming even more vulnerable to adopting secular assumptions about how to live, which leads to (5) more conformity to a culture of busyness, hurry and overload. And then the cycle begins again.[11]

Does that sound familiar to you? When I read these words, I felt like Zigarelli had been watching me on a hidden camera. He goes on to conclude that, statistically, the most common professions to get caught in this vicious cycle are doctors, lawyers, and (wait for it) *pastors*. Not the pastor writing these words, of course. Other, less mature pastors.

Carl Jung, the Swiss psychiatrist whose research is the basis of the Myers-Briggs personality test, put it bluntly: "Hurry is not *of* the Devil; it *is* the Devil."[12] The modern-day sage Richard Foster writes, "In contemporary society our Adversary [a biblical title for the devil] majors in three things: noise, hurry, and crowds. If he can keep us engaged in 'muchness' and 'manyness,' he will rest satisfied."[13] A journalist once asked theologian Thomas Merton to diagnose the leading spiritual disease of our time. Merton gave a one-word answer: "efficiency."[14]

We tend to attribute the complexity and busyness of our lives to a false culprit. We blame it on our environment. The pace of activity in our cities, our workload or office culture, our stage in life, and the current demands on our time are the assumed chief causes of our overwhelmed lives.

Quaker missionary Thomas Kelly, writing in 1941, made a different observation after spending a full year "slowing down" and "simplifying" on a twelve-month sabbatical in Hawaii. Like other Americans, he had carried with him to the tropics the "mad-cap, feverish life" he knew on the mainland.[15] Your inner life is not a mirror image of your environment. If anything, the opposite is true. We create an environment that mirrors our inner life. Kelly observed:

> Strained by the very mad pace of our daily outer burdens, we are further strained by an inward uneasiness, because we have hints that there is a way of life vastly richer and deeper than all this hurried existence, a life of unhurried serenity and peace and power. If only we could slip over into that Center! If only we could find the Silence which is the source of sound![16]

All of these teachers are circling around the same thing: hurry is the great enemy of spiritual life in our day.

I'm sure the sons of Korah want all of us to be mentally and emotionally healthy, but what's at stake isn't *only* our ability to stay centered. When this psalm urges us to "be still," it's not pushing us toward a self-care retreat; it's undermining an ancient conspiracy. All the way back at the beginning of the story, Adam and Eve took and ate the forbidden fruit from that one forbidden tree.[17] They sinned. Then they hid, made clothes, argued, and blamed. They dealt with their sin through what Richard Foster calls "muchness and manyness," what Michael Zigarelli names "busyness," and what Dallas Willard diagnoses as "hurry." And ever since then, we've always found it easiest to ignore the truth as long as we never stop moving. In the fall of humanity, we mastered the art of hurry. "And so we end up as good people, but as people who are not very deep: not bad, just busy; not immoral, just distracted; not lacking in soul, just preoccupied; not disdaining depth, just never doing the things to get us there," says Ronald Rolheiser.[18]

We try to import prayer into our hurried lives—treating the symptoms but avoiding the full detox—and the result is lip service to God, while effortlessly conforming to culture remains the one, true god we worship. We can keep up the illusion, ignore the truth—as long as we never stop moving.

Dear reader, I know how important you are. I know you've got a ton going on at work and have many demands at home. I know there are people who depend on you, a Netflix queue that needs attention, and a social media personality the internet can't live without, but can I gently remind you that the sons of Korah practiced the prayer posture of stillness, as surely did David as the king of a nation in a world of tribal warfare?

I go to bed worried about deadlines, bills, and to-do lists. David hit the pillow worried about the enemy camped in the hill country and waiting for the right moment to charge. And he prioritized time for stillness. He had a habit of stillness that allowed him to see his own life from God's perspective.

"Be still." The Latin term is *vacate*, from which we get the English word *vacation*. The invitation of prayer anytime, anywhere is this: Take a vacation. Stop playing God over your own life for a moment. Release control. Return to the created order.

Be still. Prayer begins there. But that's only the beginning.

Know God

What were you doing on August 21, 2017?

You probably won't remember just by thinking back to that date, so maybe if you hear about an event that took place, it will help jog your memory: a total solar eclipse visible from our vantage point down here on earth, an event the US hadn't seen since 1979. It was huge news. People organized viewing parties. Some took the day off from work. Others just went about their Monday routine, ticking items off their agenda while the rest of us stared at the sky.

Personally, I was excited to see it, but also uninterested enough to disregard the "you'll need to purchase these special glasses or you may go blind looking upward" announcement. So when the eclipse actually happened, I was walking down Twenty-Third Street—a particularly buzzing thoroughfare on Manhattan's West Side. Twenty-Third Street runs through the heart of Chelsea, home to New York's upscale art galleries, independent theaters, and most iconic hotel. But it's also a transportation hub, close enough to Times Square to attract tourists and chain stores and plenty of hyper-busy, perpetually angry New Yorkers trying to get from A to B. That's where I was when the moon passed between the sun and earth like someone in a crowded room slipping between two people in conversation, briefly blacking out the sunlight in the middle of the day.

It was one of those New York moments I'll remember forever. People were stopped all over the sidewalk, passing glasses back and forth. As it turned out, it didn't matter who had prepared and who hadn't. Everyone who wanted a look was getting a look, and everyone who looked was talking to one another like little kids. Sophisticated New Yorkers, momentarily returning to their inner child at a science museum on a fourth-grade field trip. That was most of us. But it wasn't everyone.

There was another group of people, equally united in defiant annoyance at everyone clogging up the sidewalk to stare at the sun. They grunted and scoffed their way through the crowd, adult children disguised in business casual, using every nonverbal means of communication imaginable to say, *I'm really, really important, and you're in my way.*

That posture of annoyance was particularly ironic in light of perspective. If you reverse the perspective—from the edge of the cosmos looking down instead of from Twenty-Third Street looking up—things look quite a bit different. From that angle, the annoyed, hustling and bustling, highly important people angling their way through the obstacle course of onlookers seem insignificant.

Our sun and moon and eight planets are just one little neighborhood among an estimated 200 billion neighborhoods that make up our universe.[19] If we think of the Milky Way galaxy as being the size of the entire continent of North America, our solar system would fit into a coffee cup.[20] Two Voyager spacecrafts are cruising toward the edge of the solar system at a rate of more than 35,000 miles per hour. They've been doing that for more than forty years and have traveled more than 11 billion miles, with no end in sight.[21] When NASA sends communication to one of those Voyagers traveling at that velocity, it takes about seventeen hours to get there.[22] That data has led scientists to estimate that to send a "speed of light" message to the edge of the universe would take more than 15 billion years to arrive.[23]

"So, yes, Chelsea art dealer, you are very important. But when we think about what we're all gazing at while you make your agitation known through grunts and mumbles, you're also impossibly young, urgently expiring, and unbelievably small."

You and I see the world with our own two eyes, and from that minuscule perspective, we tend to convince ourselves that we are (or at least should be) in control, directing our own lives, and scripting our future. We come back again to the truth that Philip Yancey reminded us of earlier in the chapter: "Prayer is the act of seeing reality from God's point of view." God is the one who calls us to "be still, and know that I am God."

Psalm 8 marvels at this very wonder:

When I consider your heavens,
the work of your fingers,
the moon and the stars,
which you have set in place,
what is mankind that you are mindful of them,
human beings that you care for them? (vv. 3–4)

All of our scientific discoveries in the thousands of years since this simple prayer was written have only confirmed its wisdom. In the vast expanse, who is this God who would concern himself with the likes of *me*? The great scandal and most important work of prayer is simply to let ourselves be loved by God.

There's a good kind of small, and it comes with wonder at the God who is big enough to fashion the cosmos with his breath and personal enough to take a real interest in the events of my day and the fluctuation of my emotions.

I love cities. Gritty, bustling, diverse urban streets have been home to me for the whole of my adult life. I feel more at home on a crowded, smelly subway platform than on a rural backroad or in a suburban strip mall. But as is true for anywhere else, there are pros and cons. The way I see it, there's one obvious drawback to living in a major city—the sky above. The bright lights of the city below drown out the lights in the night sky above. Stars are mostly invisible from a city street.

Isn't there profound symbolism in the fact that our artificial lights drown out the heavenly lights? Unless you get a particularly clear, dark night, we've found a way to darken the stars, a way to pretend that all we see here on the ground is all there is. The stars are still there, but in the city—the lights of our offices that stay on late, bright advertisements vying for our attention, the yellow glow of so many lamps in so many apartment windows—it all works together to drown out the lights that remind us of how small we are. It all works together to convince me that the world from behind my tiny perspective is all there is. City dwellers are in danger of missing what David saw—our lives against the backdrop of something bigger.

What started with Adam and Eve never stopped. The same ancient conspiracy repeats itself in the Tower of Babel, in King Saul, in the Pharisaic priesthood, in the CEO of your company, and in me. We're all prone to drown out our view of God, to keep moving, to go about our lives as though we are the center.

Stillness is the quiet space where God migrates from the periphery back to the center, and prayer pours forth from the life that has God at the center.

Know Yourself

In Psalm 146, smack in the middle of a bunch of poetry praising the greatness of God, the psalmist drops the record-scratching lines, "Put not your trust in princes, in a son of man, in whom there is no salvation. When his breath departs, he returns to the earth; on that very day his plans perish."[24] At first glance, these words seem woefully out of place, like a line from a eulogy was accidentally added to a praise anthem, but seen from the right perspective, this is prayer.

Western culture is increasingly a haven for the young, who look endlessly into a future of adventure and discovery stretching out in front of them. We celebrate the first half of life—toned bodies, stylized wardrobes, vocational upward mobility, and exciting weekend plans. The elderly are a forgotten breed.

I spent twelve years in New York City. I grieved the loss of the stars, but I relished the view of the skyline. My favorite view of the Manhattan skyline was always the angle from Green-Wood

Jessica Staton

Cemetery in Brooklyn. I was always strangely comforted when I looked across all those tombstones at the city spires behind them. Every one of those stones represents someone who was living fast, making plans, and dodging every obstacle in the way of their preferred future. In other words, someone with a will who did their best to bring that will to bear on the present moment. Now they're a memory, and the city is filled with new people living even faster and making more plans.

This view has a way of reminding me that everything I'm stressed about, every conflict that's replaying in the back of my mind, every anxiety churning in my stomach, and every preoccupation I have about tomorrow morning—all of that noise one day will cease. "When his breath departs, he returns to the earth; on that very day his plans perish." Those tombstones are an important reminder of how temporary I am.

Psalm 39, another of David's prayers, reads, "Show me, LORD, my life's end and the number of my days; let me know how fleeting my life is. You have made my days a mere handbreadth; the span of my years is as nothing before you. Everyone is but a breath, even those who seem secure."[25]

By now you know what David's doing when he prays. He's undermining the most ancient conspiracy. The lie whispered just before Adam and Eve plucked the forbidden fruit was, "You will not certainly die."[26] That lie wreaked (and still wreaks) havoc on the human soul and social order.

So a prayer like "Let me know how fleeting my life is" is not self-deprecating or depressive; it's self-aware victory. To turn our fast lives into stillness and our busy minds into solitude is an act of rebellion against the curse that runs through our veins.

When we live in constant noise, we forget our mortality, and the consequences are of the furthest-reaching variety. Live like this world and this life is all you've got, and you'll lose yourself in trying to be everything for everybody. Pretending you are eternal is a miserable, dehumanizing lie—the original lie. We never tire of believing it and never fail to lose ourselves in it.

On the contrary, when, by stillness, we remember our mortality, we recover who we are. "Solitude is the furnace of transformation," says Henri Nouwen. "Without solitude we remain victims of our society and continue to be entangled in the illusions of the false self . . . Solitude is the place of the great struggle and the great encounter—the struggle against the compulsions of the false self, and the encounter with the loving God who offers himself as the substance of the new self."[27]

David was pleading with God to remind him that he is temporary, not because he was depressed but because it would show him his true value!

> What is mankind that you are mindful of them,
> human beings that you care for them?

You have made them a little lower than the angels
and crowned them with glory and honor.
(Psalm 8:4–5)

When I pray, when I see myself as I really am from God's perspective, I behold not only my own smallness but also how valuable I truly am to God. David goes on to pray things like, "God keeps count of my anxious tossing while trying to sleep and bottles up every tear I've ever shed. God's good thoughts toward me outnumber the grains of sand on the world's beaches!"[28] Where does someone get the moxie to pray like that? David is free enough to admit he's not in control, not all-powerful, not enough and doesn't have to be. He's not wallowing in his lack; he's celebrating it.

When you see how great God is and how fragile and fleeting you are, you equally see how profoundly you matter. The Creator has time *for you.* You and I are clay jars. We're dust. But God has hidden redemption in us. God has hidden away a kind of life that never stops in us. Only when you see who you really are can you also see how profoundly you matter.

"The creature only needs a certain degree of awareness of what it really is, and it will break forth into prayer," wrote nineteenth-century Swiss theologian Hans Urs von Balthasar.[29]

"Be still, and know that I am God." Slow down. Remember who God really is. Remember who you really are. That's prayer.

Unhurried Love

Jesus was intentional about his own practice of stillness. He began his ministry with forty days of wilderness solitude. He retreated into stillness before he chose the twelve disciples from his growing crowd of followers, after he healed a leper, and as he sent out his followers to minister to the surrounding villages. Frequently, he slipped away from the crowd late at night and early in the morning, usually to the Mount of Olives, which seemed to be his preferred setting for quietness. He retreated into the company of the Father from the noise of praise and criticism alike—escaping the clamor of the crowd in the face of objective success and apparent failure to listen instead to the still, small whisper of the Spirit.

Jesus was intentional, and yet he was equally interruptible.

Sure, he slipped away from the crowds, but he also allowed himself to be interrupted—mid-mission—to heal Bartimaeus on the outskirts of Jericho, a hemorrhaging woman in a crowd, and even to appreciate the faith of a Syrophoenician woman.

Jesus was intentional *and* interruptible. There's a word for that posture: *unhurried*. Hurry is the great enemy of the spiritual life. Why? Because hurry kills love. Hurry hides behind anger, agitation, and self-centeredness, blinding our eyes to the truth that we are God's beloved and she is sister, he is brother.

Throughout church history, certain sects have devoted their entire lives to stillness. The Russian church gave a name to this solitary way: *poustinia*. These radical contemplatives withdrew to the desert to live in isolation and perpetual solitude. They called themselves *poustiniki*, a term meaning "being with everybody," which seems like an odd title for a solitary life. They embraced lives of intentional stillness as a discipline, but equally lives of inter-ruptibility, refusing to ever latch their door, remaining constantly available, and making the need of their neighbor the highest prior-ity. Intentional and interruptible. Unhurried.

Stillness before God transforms us into unhurried love. It is in the stillness of silent prayer that God turns over the soil of our hearts, revealing our desires to us and the source of their fullest satisfaction. When we stop moving, stop talking, and arrive present and quiet before God, he takes all of our disordered desires, distorted attachments, and codependencies and transforms them into love.

When we use others to meet our needs, we can't love them. Codependent people don't truly love each other. They're using each other. Each needs the other to feel okay. When we need the world, need something from the world, need something from the fearfully and wonderfully made people who populate the world to make us feel whole ourselves, we can't love.

God has to break our attachments to the world so we can truly love the world. God has to break our attachments to the people in it who feed our egos so we can truly see others, know others, welcome others, and love others. The place where this work happens is silent prayer. In this way, stillness is profoundly missional. Stillness starts in isolation and ends in "being with everybody."

Prayer Posture

Almost everyone who recites Psalm 46 stops with, "Be still, and know that I am God," but that's not where the sons of Korah stopped. Be still. Let go of your anxiety. Lay down your burden. Take a rest for your soul. And then, "I will be exalted among the nations, I will be exalted in the earth."[30] That's the destination of this prayer, the promise we become aware of in holy stillness.

"Exalted in the earth" means God's presence becomes reality, plainly visible. It means love breaks out everywhere there is hate. Kindness floods competition and sweeps it away. Peace swallows up fear. Joy washes over jealousy. Self-control calms rage. Here's the way God promises to get all that done: "Be still, and know that I am God."

Be still. Remember who God is. Remember who you are. Then

do your best to live without getting the order mixed up. That'll be enough. That's where you start changing, and as a result, the world around you starts changing too.

Picture yourself on a beach. It's a brisk November day. The cold wind cuts through your clothes; waves crash melodically as water pulls in and out with the tide; the sun hangs low in the late afternoon; and the water stretches hundreds of miles beyond what looks like the edge.

See anything more powerful than you?

Great. Start there.

PRACTICE

Be Still

Many confuse stillness with waiting for revelation. Sometimes revelation does come, and it's marvelous. But that's not the purpose of stillness. The purpose is consent. It is the daily practice of consenting to the work of God's Spirit, which is deeper than understanding or words. It is how "deep calls to deep"[31] from our souls to his.

Pick a consistent time. For you, this may be the final moments before rushing off on your morning commute, the sudden silence right after dropping the kids at school, or the daily office lunch break. It could be the very first thing you do in the morning or the last thing you do before your head hits the pillow. "When" doesn't matter, so long as the "when" is consistent, because there's no such thing as a habit or priority that doesn't happen consistently.

Create a ritual. Choose an ordinary place to become sacred—ordinary holy ground. This could be your favorite chair, the back porch steps, the upstairs balcony, or the window seat in the city bus. Sit up straight with your two feet planted firmly on the ground.

Lay your hands in your lap, palms open, facing up. Close your eyes. Breathe in deeply and exhale slowly three times. Pray something simple and invitational. Traditionally, this is called a breath prayer and sounds like, "Here I am, Lord," or "Come, Holy Spirit," or "Lord, have mercy."

Then be quiet. Be still. Wait. I suggest setting a timer—a chime on your device or an old-fashioned stopwatch will do. When you set a timer, it keeps you from needing to open your eyes to check the time. Start with two minutes. Do this every day. Just two minutes of silence. After a month, bump it up to four, and then a month later to six. Keep this going until you get to ten minutes.

Resist the urge to decide if this practice of silent prayer is "working." Don't evaluate if you're "getting anything out of it." Simply trust that the practice of a couple centuries' worth of saints, and the practice of Jesus himself, might have a place in your life too. Practice silence as a sacrificial offering to God. It's that simple. It's about giving something of yourself to God, not getting something from God. One day you'll look up, discovering that somewhere along the way—at a point you can't name precisely but know for sure you've crossed—silent prayer became a lifeline, an essential.

Give God the first word, and let spoken prayer follow as a response.

Chapter 3

OUR FATHER

Adoration

"This, then, is how you should pray:

'Our Father in heaven,
hallowed be your name.'"
Matthew 6:9

They had sent hundreds of small teams on dangerous abolition assignments to free slaves from forced labor and inhumane living conditions. Now, in a plush Washington, DC, auditorium, the International Justice Mission (IJM) was holding a conference to raise awareness and advocacy for some of their most formidable justice work.

They called it a conference, but, really, it was a prayer meeting. There were no keynote speeches, no pleas for financial donations, no calls to action. This was a two-day prayer meeting. "Let's ask God to do, by supernatural means, what seems impossible—or at least impossibly slow—by natural means: free the captives in India."[1]

Wayne sat in one of those plush seats praying his guts out,

petitioning the God who calls every soul "fearfully and wonderfully made,"[2] a unique creation bearing his divine image. Wayne pleaded with God to act, to get his holy hands dirty with the urgent and tragic needs of his children. And he wasn't praying from a safe distance. Wayne himself had gotten his hands dirty with those very needs. He was an IJM employee deployed on those very abolition missions. He prayed with the power and compassion of firsthand experience.

"But here's the thing," he explained over a cup of tea in his living room one evening several years later, "the conference didn't work. Slavery is still a crisis in India. I couldn't tell any discernible difference as a result of all that prayer."

He continued, as if forming his question aloud as he went. "I've followed Jesus my whole life. As far back as I can remember, I've spoken to a God I believed was listening. I've been moved to tears and have danced with joy. But now, as an adult driven by the cause of Christ to address some of the world's harshest suffering, I have this one question I can't shake: Why wouldn't God answer that prayer?"

There it was. He had found the question he was circling like a scrawny vulture over rodent prey.

"God is all-powerful, completely loving, knows each of those slaves by name, and has numbered the hairs on their heads, right? He loves justice, hates injustice, and promises to break the yoke of oppression and set the captive free."

Wayne wasn't looking at me anymore. He stared at the old hardwood floor of his dingy Lower East Side apartment. He first addressed me, but now God was the object of his interrogation: "Here's an auditorium full of people pleading with God to do something about the suffering of his own sons and daughters. And God is either ignorant or apathetic or some intolerable combination of the two. Or, scariest of all, not listening, not there. Because if he is, well, why wouldn't God answer *that* prayer?"

If you've ever asked that question, your own version of it is likely rushing painfully back to mind now. If you haven't ever asked that question or one like it, you will. It's only a matter of time.

Pray Differently

When Jesus' disciples said to him, "Teach us to pray,"[3] Jesus wasn't responding to a bunch of novices. Prayer was the order of the disciples' lives, and it had been since the day they were born to Jewish parents in ancient Israel. If not unfamiliarity, what prompted these disciples to say, "Teach us to pray"?

Jesus prayed differently. He honored the common Jewish prayer rhythm (more on that later), but he prayed with a sense of familiarity with God that no one had ever seen. He also prayed with a reverence that was more than cultural but was sincere and honest. His prayers were conversations, not just pleas, involving as much—probably more—listening than talking. It was in prayer that Jesus got his marching orders. Prayer was the place where his eyes were opened and his steps directed. "Very truly I tell you, the Son can do nothing by himself; he can do only what he sees his Father doing."[4] Most distinctly, his prayers were effective. They got God's attention.

When Jesus taught his disciples to pray, he wasn't teaching them to pray more or pray harder, but rather to pray differently. "Teach us to pray"—the implication being, "to pray like that, the way *you* do it, Jesus."

Remember Who You're Talking To

Jesus responded to his disciples' question, not with instructions, but with a demonstration. He showed them how to pray, offering a model to follow. And here's the first bit, the first movement of prayer the Jesus way: "Our Father in heaven, hallowed be your name."[5] In that turn of phrase, Jesus lays a threefold foundation for prayer:

1. Remember who God is.
2. Remember who you are.
3. Remember who we are to each other.

Remember Who God Is

Calling God "Father" is dismissible today. It rolls off the tongue as unconsciously as the lyrics of "Happy Birthday" as you carry a candlelit cake to the dinner table. It's become just cheesy enough to edge past in search of some more sophisticated insight from Jesus in the lines that follow. Worse yet, for some its use is grouped in with a centuries-long patriarchal history of male superiority and female oppression.

But the disciples likely gasped when Jesus said it. The temple that served as the training ground for their prayers had taught them to pray with supreme reverence. The grounding text for the Jewish people's understanding of God was the book of Exodus—when the Lord appeared to the people in the form of a cloud by day and fire by night.[6] The big question in ancient days wasn't, "Does God exist?" It would be foolish to ask such a question. "Of course God exists! Open your eyes, man! He's the cylindrical pillar of fire stretching from the desert floor into the night sky and serves as our trail guide!" Instead, the existential question in ancient days was, "Is God *knowable*?" Because a pillar of fire doesn't provoke doubt, but neither does it provide intimacy.

These disciples knew a God of cleansing rituals and animal sacrifices, a God of ten plagues and blood on the doorpost, a God who parts seas and floods the earth, a God with a heavy hand of deliverance and a heavy hand of judgment—awesome in power but hard to get to know. Jesus did nothing to diminish the reverence, nothing to minimize the power of God. Jesus made that powerful God knowable.

Jesus didn't introduce them to a new God. He was abundantly clear about that. "I have not come to abolish them [the Law or the Prophets] but to fulfill them."[7] Jesus prayed to the revered God of power and judgment with the familiarity of the term *Father*.

It was an attractive scandal. Scandalous for all the obvious reasons. "How dare you! Do you know who you're talking to!" Attractive for all the obvious reasons. "God is knowable. And this man Jesus knows exactly who he is, exactly who he's talking to."

The reverence of ancient Israel is extinct in the modern West. We live without sacredness, yawning at the very words that made the disciples gasp. Our world is a million miles from theirs. Our hearts, though, are the same.

Now in my second decade in pastoral ministry I can say confidently that the number one obstacle the modern person faces when it comes to prayer is an inability to receive the love of God. We struggle to believe in a God as powerful, good, knowable, and loving as the one Jesus introduces us to. "God is love."[8] It's who he is, the summary of his character boiled down to a single, defining word. We buy that intellectually, but at a deeper level, somewhere in our emotions, in our bones, we don't trust it.

In Genesis 3, when the serpent tempts Eve, his strategy is telling. "Did God really say, 'You must not eat from any tree in the garden'?"[9] It's interesting to note that at no point does the serpent's temptation become direct. Never does he say, "Here, try the fruit," or anything of that sort. Instead, the serpent takes aim at Eve's belief in the character of God.

God says to Adam and Eve, "You are free to eat from any tree in the garden; but you must not eat from the tree of the knowledge of good and evil, for when you eat from it you will certainly die."[10]

Turn the page, and the serpent repeats the command, with some key adjustments in tone and emphasis. "Did God really say, 'You must not eat from any tree in the garden'?" This is the most effective kind of lie because there are seeds of truth in it. It's not an outright fallacy but a twisting of the truth, a deception. In Genesis 2, God displayed his generosity, offering free reign over the garden: "*Any* tree . . . except this one; it's poisonous." The enemy flips that command from broad and generous to narrow and restrictive. "Did God really say you can't eat from any tree in the garden?" He's flipping the command to make a generous offer seem stingy. He's not asking Eve to eat the fruit; he's chipping away at her trust in God.

There's something else going on here, something technical but important. In Genesis 2, God is repeatedly called *Yahweh Elohim* ("Lord God," in English). But every time the serpent refers to God, he just says *Elohim* ("God"), the abstract name for divinity, dropping the personal. It's calling someone by their title instead of their name—Doctor instead of Susan, Professor instead of Darrell, Sir instead of Dad. It's respectful, but distant, depersonalized. The more intimacy in a relationship, the less likely someone is to be known by a title. An MD's spouse doesn't call her "Doctor"; he calls her by her first name. My kids don't call me "Pastor"; they call me Dad. The serpent subtly demotes God from Father to a distant, stingy dictator. Mighty in power, sure, but unknowable, untrustable.

Eve takes the bait. She remembers in the narrow, demanding light of the serpent what God said intimately and generously.

Protestants typically call Jesus' exemplary prayer "the Lord's Prayer," while Catholics simply name it the "Our Father." I wonder if Catholics are onto something. Because every line of the prayer flows from here: "Our Father." It all starts and ends with remembering who we're talking to.

Remember Who You Are

Eve didn't only forget who God is; she lost her own identity as well. When she imagined God as something less than "Father," she in turn imagined herself as something less than "daughter."

Adoration given to God is always given back to us. As we lift our eyes, recovering a true view of God's identity, we also recover his view of us. The biblical letters do not call the earliest Christ followers "Christians"; they had another title: "saints." Today, we tend to reserve that title for the most pious spiritual elite. But in the early church, it was commonplace, the everyday name for the everyday Jesus follower. That's because the biblical use of the word *saint* has nothing to do with human competence and everything to do with divine grace.

To call someone a saint is not to necessarily call them good; it is only to name them as someone who has experienced the goodness of God.[11] We recover our sainthood simply through adoration. When we remember who God is, when we experience his goodness, we recover our own identity as well.

I find the English novelist Reynolds Price's definition helpful: "A saint is someone who—with however many faults, even crimes—leads us by example, almost never by words, to imagine the hardest thing of all: the seamless love of God for all creation, including ourselves."[12] Adoration is the place of prayer where we discover that God's love is the defining reality of every square inch of creation, including me and you.

"Oh, magnify the LORD with me, and let us exalt his name together!" writes the author of Psalm 34.[13] And when we magnify the Lord's name, he reminds us of our own name—*saint*.

Following his exemplary prayer, Jesus expounds on God's generosity, hammering God's true identity into our imaginations. "If you, then, though you are evil, know how to give good gifts to your children, how much more will your Father in heaven give good gifts to those who ask him!"[14] According to Jesus, God *wants* to bless you. Did that sink in? God *wants* to bless you. His predisposition toward you is generosity. He loves to give you what you need and even what you want.

My four-year-old son, Hank, reminds me daily, "You'll always love me no matter what, though, Dad." Sometimes he says it just after I've dished out consequences for some unacceptable behavior. Other times it'll be at random—when I'm setting a dinner plate in front of him or dropping him off at school or tucking him in at night. "You'll always love me no matter what, though, Dad." He won't let me get through a day without reminding me at least once. Or is he asking me? It's hard to tell. I think it's both. "Yep. That's right, buddy," I reply. "No matter what." And we both remember who we are to each other.

We grow up in a thousand different ways. We become more sophisticated, more responsible, more introspective. The raw physicality of our adolescence grows into self-control. The unbridled, hormonal emotion of our youth stabilizes as we enter adulthood. The pleas and demands for our childish way mature into social norms with time. We grow up, and that's a good thing.

But our hearts are Peter Pan—forever young, never growing up. We never outgrow the need to be reminded by the day, by the hour, sometimes even by the minute, "You'll always love me no matter what, though, Dad." Because the second we forget that, the second it's diluted into a trope or held in the intellect while a story of our sufficiency or control or performance lives in our bones, our lives unravel, and so does our faith.

When we call God our Father, we are equally remembering that we are completely, uniquely loved. Until we know that love, nothing can truly be right within us, but after that simple revelation, something becomes irrevocably right within us at the deepest level. When we pray, "Our Father," we are really asking him to remind us again today that we are loved.

Remember Who We Are to Each Other

When our trust in God erodes, so does our intimacy with others. Adam and Eve, once "naked and unashamed,"[15] instinctively started covering up with fig leaves. When Jesus taught his disciples to pray, the scandal wasn't only the name he chose for God. He didn't teach them to pray to "my Father." He said, "Our Father," a claim about not only who we are to God but equally who we are to one another— sister and brother. All of us, siblings in one family, one bloodline.

I so easily forget the sacredness of the people I encounter in my everyday routine, treating them as extras in the background of a feature film in which I play the lead. My wife and children, the coworkers at my office, the people I meet with, the people I briskly rush past on the sidewalk and sit next to on the city bus—all of them, extras. When our trust in God is fractured, so is our intimacy with one another.

Prayer is the place I recover God's true identity, my own, and, equally, the identity of everyone else. As Brennan Manning said so pointedly, "If I am not in touch with my own belovedness, then I cannot touch the sacredness of others."[16]

We forget who God is to us, and we forget who we are to one another. Prayer is the place our memory is restored. All of our praying and all of our doing emerge from a recovery of identity—God's, mine, his, and hers.

Hallowed Be Your Name

The word *hallowed* means "to make holy," or "to set apart, sanctify, consecrate, dedicate." The closest commonly used English word is probably *honor.* "Our Father" is a reminder of God's intimacy; "hallowed" is a reminder of his separateness, his majesty, his incomprehensible greatness.

The pendulum of popular thought has swung between Jesus' time and our own. We are comforted by the sentimentality of "our Father," a title that scandalized the ancient world, but we are equally scandalized by the devoted deference of "hallowed be your name," words that would've comforted the ancients. And it is for this precise reason that we need the second line of the Lord's Prayer every bit as much as the ancients needed the first.

Hallowing is an active kind of praying—honoring, adoring, naming the greatness of God. Jesus teaches that when our lips open from the quiet, centering place of contemplative silence, the words we speak first should honor the God who is on the receiving end of our prayers.

Hallowed. Why start there? Why does an all-powerful, completely loving, wholly self-sufficient God need me, a meager creation of his own imagination, to tell him how great he is? Is he honestly that insecure? Is God a cosmic megalomaniac who loves to read and reread his own press clippings? Is he so easily manipulated that a little buttering up before the big ask will do the trick? Not even close.

In fact, this "hallowing" business isn't for *God's* benefit at all; it's for *my own* benefit, and yours. For my prayer to have any sense of coherence, I need to start by "hallowing" because our prayers come from the setting of the world.

Subconsciously, I tend to believe the world is a neutral place. It's not! The world is a contested place where, almost always, a name other than Jesus is being worshiped. When you and I open our mouths and begin to pray, almost certainly, another name is being hallowed in our hearts—the names of accomplishment, success, productivity, approval from another person, comfort, easy execution of our own plans, self-will in all its destructive varieties. When we pray, we step out of the fundamental reality of the world and into the fundamental reality of God, so we must begin by inviting God to reorder our affections.

The apostle John had a revelatory vision of heaven and wrote it down. It's the final book in the Bible, and I'll be honest, it's pretty far out there.

In the center, around the throne, are four living creatures; each has six wings and is covered with eyes all over its body, even under its wings. Day and night they never stop saying, "Holy, holy, holy is the Lord God Almighty, who was, and is, and is to come."[17]

Covered with eyes—front to back, even under the wings? That's bizarre, isn't it? It's kind of gross even. But God is the designer of every creature. He gave fish gills so they could breathe underwater, and birds wings so they could fly through the air. So what is the function of all these eyes? To see. Their purpose is to hallow God's name, so he gave them as many eyes as possible so they could fully see him.

And seeing God as he really is leads to a chorus of unceasing, eternal hallowing: "Holy, holy, holy is the Lord God Almighty, who was, and is, and is to come." They never get over it, never grow tired or bored, never get too sophisticated for the wonder of God. And neither do we.

Adoration is not always the overflow of our hearts. In fact, it rarely is. It is an act of rebellion against the empty promises of this world and of defiance in the face of circumstances.

Prayer flows from the posture of our hearts toward God, not from reaction to the world around us. Everything that comes from the Lord's Prayer after this first movement is an overflow of the name of God being hallowed in the heart of the praying person.

"Teach us to pray," the disciples say to Jesus. And he responds, in essence, "Start by remembering who you're talking to." Biblically, we are commanded to "remember" more frequently than to "obey," "do," "not do," "go," or even "pray." Remember. Because in the long journey of the spiritual life, we tend to forget. We tend to lose the plot of our own redemption story. When Jesus teaches us to pray, he picks up on that same thread. "Remember who you're talking to."

Remember who God is.

Remember who you are.

Remember who we are to each other.

Defiant Adoration

"Why wouldn't God answer *that* prayer?" Wayne stared into the hardwood floor of his dingy apartment living room, likely picturing the nameless faces of so many still enduring the conditions of slavery in India. The weight of his honesty hung in the air between us.

It's a straightforward question that doesn't have a short, straightforward answer. It's a question we'll continue to unpack in the chapters ahead. What we know for sure at this point is that powerful prayer begins with adoration—adoration when it flows from our lips effortlessly and adoration when it's gritty, willful, even defiant.

In Acts 16, Paul and Silas were on their way to a prayer meeting when they healed a trafficked girl desperately in need of help, and the men using her for profit had them locked up on a bogus charge. So instead of leading a prayer meeting in the temple, they were likely publicly stripped and beaten with rods and then held in the ancient version of solitary confinement—the innermost cell, with their backs pinned against the cold stone wall, hands and ankles chained so tightly they could barely shift their weight.

And then, quite unexpectedly, the Bible tells us, "About midnight Paul and Silas were praying and singing hymns to God, and the other prisoners were listening to them."[18]

Praying and singing hymns? Are these guys delusional? No. Quite the opposite actually. They understand the power of defiant adoration. They start to sing—and it's not because they're suddenly caught up in a moment of euphoria, inspiration, and wonder. "Hallowed be your name" is a longing to see God here and now, to know his presence in the midst of this mess. They start to sing as a way of praying, "Where are you, God? We want to see you. You are the loving Father. You promise to be a shelter in chaos, the calm in the raging storm, freedom for the captive! So be who you say you are. Show yourself here." That's the subtext beneath the a cappella hymn session coming from the innermost cell.

It's defiant adoration. And that's the most potent kind. "It is relatively easy to meet God in moments of joy or bliss. In these situations we correctly count ourselves blessed by God," observes psychologist David Benner. "The challenge is to believe that this is also true—and to know God's presence—in the midst of doubt, depression, anxiety, conflict, or failure. But the God who is Immanuel is equally in those moments we would never choose as in those we would always gladly choose."[19] "Hallowed be your name" is always most powerful in the most unlikely places.

The story goes on: "Suddenly there was such a violent earthquake that the foundations of the prison were shaken. At once all the prison doors flew open, and everyone's chains came loose."[20]

One thing led to another, and by the time the sun rose the following morning, the prison warden had experienced salvation, and his entire family had been baptized in his own bathtub. Paul and Silas opened their mouths to hallow in the midst of an absolute mess. "I can't make sense of this chapter in the story. I want to see you here, Father." And God showed himself at midnight in prison. When they sang in a jail cell, they were dragging heaven into a dark corner of earth, and it changed the atmosphere.

The words of Jesus' teaching prayer that follow "hallowed be your name" are "your kingdom come, your will be done, on earth as it is in heaven."[21] God's kingdom often evokes thoughts of justice, salvation, and healing. But hallowing is one of the most obvious ways we bring heaven to earth.

PRACTICE

Remember Who You're Talking To

Having stilled our bodies and souls, giving God the first word, we now break the silence with adoration, remembering the God we're talking to on the other side of our simple prayers. There are several ways to do this, and they're all equally good.

Musical Worship

Many find the most effective language for the prayer of adoration to be song. A melody incorporates both intellect and emotion, both head and heart. We state truths about who God is with our minds, and we join our emotions to our intellect through music. Song allows us to speak to God with our whole being—mind, will, and emotions. A simple chorus such as, "Worthy of It All," or, "Come, Lord Jesus, Come," often changes what we pray or how we pray it.

Pray a Psalm

The hymnal of ancient Israel is found right in the middle of the Bible. Here we find the 150 psalms—prayers that have given language to generations of our spiritual ancestors. Read a psalm slowly (I prefer to read aloud, even when I'm alone). When you reach a line that resonates, allow it to be a springboard for your own prayers. Let a single verse or phrase from an ancient prayer become a foundation for praising God as Creator, Redeemer, Savior, or Friend.

Gratitude

A simple and effective form of adoration is the intentional practice of gratitude.

Historically in the Christian tradition, the prayer of examen has provided an effective framework for gratitude. Typically prayed in the evening, examen begins by reviewing the day with God, playing back the events of the day like a movie and thanking God for every good thing along the way—the first sip of coffee that morning, the moment of laughter with your daughter, the insightful conversation with a colleague, the progress made on a big project, and on and on it goes. Next, invite the Holy Spirit to illuminate the day, showing you the moment when God's presence felt nearest and the moment his presence felt most distant. While God is always with us, our awareness of his presence wanes. Finally, pray a simple prayer of intercession for tomorrow.

Chapter 4

SEARCH ME AND KNOW ME

Confession

You have searched me, Lord,
and you know me.
Psalm 139:1

October 31, 1995. It was Halloween. I was a second grader boarding the school bus and dreaming of a month's supply of candy. I happened to grab a seat next to a neighbor, who was in kindergarten at the time.

I was carrying a good deal of pride that day because I had recently completed my first ever chapter book from cover to cover. The Scholastic Book Fair had rolled through sometime in September. Somehow that little setup of cardboard cutouts in the library was like a mirage in the desert. Never were elementary schoolers so thirsty to read, mark their page with a super-cool bookmark, and pick just the right obnoxiously large, loudly colorful cap eraser for their No. 2 pencil. I was no different. When the

Scholastic Book Fair was in town, I was briefly transformed into a bookworm with a fire burning in me that only well-written fiction could satisfy.

With Halloween around the corner, naturally, I picked out the latest offering from the Goosebumps franchise. Later that day in class, I leafed forward to see how many pages were left in chapter 1. I was on page 3 and already growing bored, wondering if I had the stamina for this journey of adolescent horror. As fate would have it, at that very moment, Jacquelin approached my desk with about five books in hand. "Tyler, what chapter are you on?"

"Chapter 1. I just started."

"Oh, great. I love chapter books [that's what she called them]. Let me know if you like it."

It was at that precise moment I was certain I did possess the stamina for this horror journey. I had a crush on Jacquelin. Secretly, I suspect every boy in the class did. And if this book was the way to a lengthier interaction, I was ready to run a bubble bath, light a few aromatherapy candles, brew a cup of chamomile tea, and settle in for a sophisticated evening with my first ever "chapter book."

I finished it several weeks later. Jacquelin never asked me about it again. I went back to television immediately after.

But then Halloween rolled around. I sat down on the bus, turned to the kid next to me, and asked, "Want to hear a ghost story?"

"Sure."

Over the next fifteen minutes, I proceeded to recount every detail of that Goosebumps plot in accordance with my memory. I wrapped up just as we made it to his stop, a couple blocks before mine.

By the time I opened my front door, his mom had already called my mom with the news. "Your son told my son a ghost story, and he was so afraid that he came in shaking and crying."

I have a vivid recollection of that day because it's the first time I can remember feeling a deep sense of guilt. Something I had done with honest intentions, without aim to scare or hurt, had produced pain in the life of another. How could that be?

In high school, I had a temper so bad I was prone to outbursts. I got so angry at my younger brother that I punched a hole in the wall of my own bedroom. We never got it fixed. Just covered it with a Bob Dylan poster and pretended it didn't happen.

In college, I was out on my own for the first time, which brought all of my buried insecurities to the surface. The most effective means I found for wrapping security around my suddenly exposed and fragile sense of self was gossip. As long as I stayed on the side of mocking others behind their backs, I felt alright, comfortable in my own skin, included and accepted.

In my early twenties, I dealt with a pornography addiction. I call it an addiction, not a "struggle," because it went well beyond the bounds of my willpower. I didn't want to do it, but there I was, in my dorm room in Bible college, right after finishing up an essay on Romans, googling something on my laptop again.

That didn't just go away when I became a pastor, by the way.

I can also recall, in equally vivid detail, the heavy blanket of shame I wrapped myself in on Wednesday nights as a young youth pastor when, after preaching sermons to middle and high school students, I'd find myself staring lustfully at the glow of my iPhone screen before falling asleep. I can remember praying theologically misguided, but completely sincere prayers such as, "God, please don't penalize those kids because of my failure."

It didn't go away when I got married either.

Your fiancée discovering unflattering searches on your internet history is one thing. That follow-up conversation is awful. But confessing that you still find yourself typing those same words into those same search engines a year into marriage is another. And unlocking your phone to see that she left the internet history open, knowing she snuck a moment to check up on you, is another thing entirely. It's at that point you realize that your "struggle" has ripped distrust through the relationship you care about most and produced pain and insecurity in the person you love dearly.

Confession, and the feelings of guilt and shame that often precede it, get less cute as you grow up. When a misguided Goosebumps recap matures into marital fracture, it doesn't read nearly as charming.

It's been more than a decade since any form of disembodied lust was a struggle for me on any level. I've found what Scripture calls "victory" in that area of my life. And I've also found that God has flooded my life with people who have been right in the thick of an identical secret struggle because it's our wounds that God often uses to heal others, not our competencies.

As of this moment, it's impatience and anger that have a hold on me, which has the potential to sound okay if you keep it general (a well-cultivated habit of Christian pastors), but if you were in the room for some of the petty arguments I've started with my wife or some of the moments in which rage spilled out of me, directed at my toddler-aged children, it wouldn't seem so general.

Ten days prior to this writing, the community I pastor gathered for midnight prayer and worship to start an incredible season of twenty-four hours a day, seven days a week, unceasing prayer. "Revival, right! Come on!"

But that very day I yelled at my son, Hank, three separate times, and I had promised myself I wasn't gonna use that form of discipline anymore because, for me, it's about me releasing my anger, not about teaching him.

And in the minutes before I walked through the church door for that first midnight hour of prayer, I was walking down the sidewalk in an argument with Kirsten because I so mishandled a moment of vulnerability on her part. Now she's in tears because my response was the worst possible response.

"Revival, right! Come on!" No, I showed up that night defeated and in need.

"Merciful God, meet me here with your mercy." That's what I was whispering under my breath in the front row of the prayer meeting I was leading. And God did meet me, not because of me, but in spite of me.

I need you to unequivocally know, dear reader, that I am on the confessor side of this equation, not the absolver side. You probably already know there is nothing different about me and you when it comes to the need to confess. But it's important for you to know that I know that too.

Confession Is a Slow Dance

Picture yourself at a wedding reception with a bunch of friends (but no date), tearing up the dance floor to the tune of Ariana Grande, Justin Bieber, and a crowd-pleasing throwback from Salt-N-Pepa. If you're having that kind of night, confession is the deejay slowing things down with "The Way You Look Tonight" or a track from Al Green's deep cuts. "It's not surprising. I figured we were going here, but I'm not particularly excited about it. I'll use this four-minute window to catch my breath and refresh my beverage."

Psalm 24 is a song, composed by David, for the sake of celebration. It begins, "The earth is the LORD's, and everything in it, the world, and all who live in it; for he founded it on the seas and established it on the waters."[1] And it concludes in the repeated declaration, "Lift up your heads, you gates; be lifted up, you ancient doors, that the King of glory may come in. Who is this King of glory? The LORD strong and mighty, the LORD mighty in battle."[2] It's a triumphant crowd-pleaser, which is what makes these lines from verses 3 and 4 seem so out of place: "Who may ascend the mountain of the LORD? Who may stand in his holy place? The one who has clean hands and a pure heart, who does not trust in an idol or swear by a false god."[3] Comparatively speaking, those lines are a bit of a downer, wouldn't you agree? It's the deejay switching to a slow jam and the dance floor clearing out.

David has a habit of doing this. He is the author of most of the psalms, and he writes plenty of hits, but he tends always to sneak in a line or two or three that a savvy record label would've cut. The subtext is, "Who may ascend the mountain of the Lord? The one with clean hands and a pure heart . . . *and that's not me.*" I imagine David whispered that line in defeat so many times before he sang it loudly and triumphantly. David wanted the presence of God more than anything. Which meant that he was washed in God's holiness and at the same time confronted by his own fallenness.

If it's the presence of the living God you want, confession is part of the deal—a really good part of the deal.

Controversial Agreement

Sin is simultaneously the most controversial idea in Christianity and the one most universally agreed upon, even outside the church.

In his seminal work titled *Orthodoxy*, G. K. Chesterton called "sin" the only part of Christian theology that can really be proved.[4] Two years after that statement, Chesterton published another book, this one titled *What's Wrong with the World?* The year was 1910, and there was plenty of talk of social progress in the West. He added his own voice to that "progressive" conversation, stating in summary, "You're after the right things, but you're ignoring a key part of the diagnosis." "What's wrong with the world?" was his question, and his answer was simply this: *I am wrong.*[5] *I'm* what's wrong with the world. The world doesn't get sorted out unless I do. And that is actually not a primitive, conservative religious idea. Freud, Plato, Martin Luther King Jr., Gandhi, and Jesus all agreed on that point, just to name a handful. Everyone agrees there's something wrong with the world—everyone. The difference in philosophies and religions often comes down to what vocabulary is used to describe the world's brokenness and the way this brokenness gets mended. Sin is the precise point where historical eras, cultures, and philosophies all find agreement.

Sin is also hugely controversial. It's been so abused and manipulated over the years that, for some, the moment this tiny three-letter word appears on the page, it is minimized to a single, subjective, and often very legitimately painful experience.

The biblical idea of sin is not simple. It's massively broad. Bible scholars have pointed to eight different Hebrew words used in the Bible, all translated with the one English word *sin*. The broad biblical definition is given in the form of a story, not a statement.

In the Bible's opening pages, man and woman are described as naked and unashamed.[6] That's about a lot more than physical nudity or hippie liberation; it's about the state of their souls.

Flip the page, and the story turns on what's commonly referred to as "the fall." Sin plunges into human history.

Believing in the existence of God has never really been the hang-up for us humans. Across cultures and eras, the existence of something bigger than us has always been the popular opinion. Even today, in a post-Enlightenment, highly skeptical society bent on deconstruction, the majority of people believe in some kind of deity who is running the show.

The hang-up is, and has always been, trusting the God we believe exists. Pretty early on in the story, Adam and Eve started to suspect that God was holding out on them. They plucked the forbidden fruit in an attempt to get to a full, abundant, happy life apart from God. They trusted themselves, not the God they believed in. And that is what the Bible calls sin—good desire channeled through the wrong means. Sin is shorthand for any attempt to meet our deep needs by our own resources.[7]

The instinctive human response to sin is hiding. Right away, Adam and Eve realized they were naked and sewed fig leaves together to hide from each other. When they heard God's footsteps approaching, they even hid from God in the brush. "Naked and unashamed" instantly became "covered and ashamed." God sees them hiding (honestly, tough guy to play hide-and-seek with), and the bottom falls out of his stomach, verbalized in two questions: "Where are you?"[8] There's a long interpretive tradition in Judaism and early Christianity that sees this first question as an invitation to confession, an invitation Adam and Eve don't take, leading to a second question.[9] "Who told you that you were naked?"[10] Said another way, God is asking, "Who stole my children's innocence?"

This observation is paramount and so frequently misconstrued: Sin, defined by the biblical imagination, is not an accusation or a condemnation; it's just a diagnosis. It's a trip to the doctor's office where you describe your symptoms and discover that "there's a name for this disease." The trouble with disease is that it gets in the way of doing what we were made to do—namely, live free, healthy lives, using our bodies according to their design.

The issue with sin isn't that God has a tight moral grid, and coloring within the lines is how we prove we're on his side. It's that sin inhibits us from doing what we were made to do best—love—to receive love and to give it. Why does sin interfere with love? Because, as Eugene Peterson defines it, "Sin is a refused relationship with God that spills over into a wrong relationship with others."[11] Sin is always personal, and it's always against God. The way our sin hurts others is the collateral of that first refusal. As David prays, "Against you,

you only, have I sinned and done what is evil in your sight."[12] We do not sin against a rule or a law; we sin against our Father.

Back to the drama of Genesis 3. The heartbreaking scene ends with the statement, "[God] placed on the east side of the Garden of Eden cherubim and a flaming sword flashing back and forth to guard the way to the tree of life."[13] The entrance back into the full, free, abundant kind of life God made us for is guarded. Adam and Eve left the garden walking east, but they don't go alone; God goes with them. He's not lowering the standard of holiness, but he is coming after us. The biblical story isn't one of a compromising God; it's one of a pursuing God.

From there, the rest of the Bible is mostly picture after picture of God's pursuing love. Here's a summary of the whole sixty-six book compilation if you want to save yourself some time: I've got good news and bad news. The good news is that you are loved—loved right now without qualification or restriction, loved unconditionally for who you are, loved in a way you can't lose. The bad news is that you find it very hard to believe that and even harder to experience it. Your instinct is, and will forever be, to try to drum up your own lovableness, to become lovable in some way you can define and control, to try to become in your own eyes what you already are in God's. The good news is called grace; the bad news is called sin.

I know, painfully and personally, what it feels like to all of a sudden be aware of my need for forgiveness. Falling on my face defeated while accusing voices pound away inside my skull, and I know they're right. I am not a man of "clean hands and a pure heart."[14] My real life is a mockery of who I want to be and wish I was. And there in the midst of my exposed shame, I hear the rabbi whisper to me what he whispered to the adulterous woman: "Neither do I condemn you."[15] That love I can't seem to outrun—it's the only thing powerful enough to change me.

What if every time I find myself facedown in shame, it's an opportunity to again hear his voice say, "Neither do I condemn you"? What if the parts of our stories we'd like to erase become in the end the parts we tell forever? What if when you find yourself there, it isn't an opportunity to clean yourself up but instead to see yourself as you really are, as he's always seen you, and still hear him call you "beloved"?

God didn't lower the standard of holiness. He found a way to make us holy that isn't dependent on our performance. Grace wins.

Co-suffering

Most theological expositions of the meeting point between our sin and God's forgiveness are 100 percent true but are presented in such a way that they're stripped of all the emotion, all the heart. The Bible offers us a God who is emotional, even moved to action by his emotions. In fact, our emotions are a reflection of our heavenly Father's. That doesn't mean every emotion we feel is good. It means there's a *way to feel* every emotion that's good, that reflects God's character. Salvation doesn't diminish our sense of anger, sadness, hope, passion, or desire. God's end game isn't to make us into robots that execute flawlessly but feel nothing. Salvation redeems every human emotion as a reflection of God's divine image.

When you and I act with conviction, when we really mean something, it rarely emerges from a carefully considered, purely intellectual course of action. We live deepest from the gut, not the head. The love I have for my child, the way I felt during the first dance at my wedding, the doubled-over weight I've held as I stared into the casket of a lost loved one, the laughter that came as I watched my niece open a gift on Christmas morning—none of that emerges from an intellectual equation I've solved. It comes from somewhere deeper, somewhere more instinctive, some emotional place, something like my gut.

God has an instinctive, gut-level response to our sin and the havoc it wreaks on our lives. He is not cool and calculated. Scripture presents God with a deeper, more personal, emotional response to our condition. The author of Hebrews describes Jesus' response to sin as empathy: "For we do not have a high priest who is unable to empathize with our weaknesses, but we have one who has been tempted in every way, just as we are—yet he did not sin."[16]

The Greek word translated in the NIV as "empathize" is the compound word *sympatheo*. It is a combination of the Greek word *pascho*, meaning "to suffer" and the prefix *sun* ("with"), much like we used the prefix co- in English. This word, translated literally, means "co-suffer." That's how Jesus deals with our sin. He suffers with us—suffers the consequences of our thoughts, actions, and disordered desires; suffers the subtle agony of hiding and pretending and presenting a preferred self that traps us in perpetual insecurity; suffers the estrangement from God we willfully choose by "managing" a sin pattern we've grown tired of confessing rather than bringing it into the light of his inexhaustible love.

Our intuitive assumption is that we are closest to God when things are going well. Jesus is by my side, present and helping, when I'm living wisely and virtuously, keeping in step with his mission in me and in the world. The author of Hebrews says the exact opposite. Jesus is nearest to us in "our *weaknesses*," not our strengths. Our hearts, corrupted by sin, are like the poles of a magnet that push away, ever resistant to grace. Jesus' heart, uncorrupted, works exactly the *opposite* way. He is drawn to our sin, not intellectually like a mathematician who has worked this equation in a thousand different ways and knows that grace is the only solution that satisfies the variables. It's *instinctual*. From his gut, his primal instinct, Jesus wants to run to us in our weaknesses, to meet us there.

Empathy most often emerges from shared experience. We empathize with the weak when their weakness matches our own experience. The same is true for Jesus. Here is the source of his empathy: "[Jesus] has been tempted in every way, just as we are—yet he did not sin."[17] Jesus is a healer, yes, but he's the kind of doctor who has dealt with the same disease. He's a doctor treating lung cancer who also had lung cancer, felt the effects, and even donated one of his lungs for a transplant, so you're talking to a doctor with experiential compassion for what you're going through and a wounded body from a battle with the same symptoms. Don't you see the profound difference in that healer? The care, sincere concern, and unhurried presence of that doctor compared to the one who just dishes out prescriptions?

One of the names thrown around for Jesus is the great physician. But a doctor can't heal you without an accurate diagnosis. If you show up to a great doctor and describe yourself as "generally sick," they're not gonna be able to do a lot for you. To confess is to say, "I want to name my symptoms, completely and comprehensively, because I want healing, completely and comprehensively."

Confession, Discovered

The scandalous grace of the Great High Priest is impossible to discover in the abstract. It must come as close as personal experience. When insecurity has you pinned on your back and struggling to breathe, one of your relationships shatters, you slip on your climb toward assumed significance, you're overlooked, misunderstood, or betrayed by someone you trust—it's precisely there that Jesus is drawn instinctively to be with you, to feel the sting, to offer his healing presence, to empathize with your weakness and mine.

He shares in my pain, takes on my condition—*yet he did not sin.* And that's our hope, our only hope. The one full of the deepest empathy is equally full of healing power. He is with us in our weakness always.

How do we take Jesus up on his power to heal? Confession. Confession is how we turn to him, look him in the eye, and acknowledge his presence here with us, not to judge, but to rescue. Dane Ortlund, a Chicago area–based pastor and author, writes, "If you are in Christ, you have a Friend who, in your sorrow, will never lob down a pep talk from heaven. He cannot bear to hold himself at a distance. Nothing can hold him back. His heart is too bound up with yours."[18]

In *Lit*, Mary Karr's third installment in a brilliant trilogy of memoirs, she recalls the precise point in her life when her drinking had gotten so bad, and had been that way for so long, that she had a complete breakdown and checked herself into a mental hospital.

The first night there, so anxious she wants to crawl out of her own skin, she gets up in the middle of the night and goes into the bathroom, the only place she's allowed to be alone, unobserved. There she falls on her knees, and for the first time in her life, she does something she thought was only for the unbearably religious and unrealistically superstitious—she prays.

First, she unleashes a series of pent-up, angry, and accusatory questions she has held toward God for as long as she can remember, the "if you're really listening, where were you when . . ." sort of thing.

Finally, at the end of that list of grievances and out of breath, she begins to whisper in gratitude. "Thanks for my husband, maybe somehow he'll still take me back after all this. Thanks for my son, Dev, who was so sick as an infant, but made it through." And as she's saying it, it hits her. "I only came to the end of myself because someone needed me to keep it together, and I couldn't."[19]

Karr writes, "By checking into the hospital, I've said in some deep way *uncle* . . . I've stopped figuring so hard and begun to wait, sometimes with increasing hope, to be shown. Then it hits me. I'm actually kneeling before a toilet. The throne, as other drunks call it. How many drunken nights and slungover mornings did I worship at this altar, emptying myself of poison. And yet to pray to something above me, something invisible, had—before now—seemed degrading."[20]

On her knees, head resting on a toilet seat belonging to a rehab center, undressed of everything she had convinced everyone else she was, finally naked before God. And in her nakedness, her shame was being washed in divine love.

Eugene Peterson writes, "God does not deal with sin by ridding our lives of it as if it were a germ, or mice in the attic. God does not deal with sin by amputation as if it were a gangrenous leg, leaving us crippled, holiness on a crutch. God deals with sin by forgiving us, and when he forgives us there is more of us, not less."[21]

David discovered the healing power of forgiveness, and that discovery turned confession from a slow dance to a victory dance. "You have searched me, LORD, and you know me," he wrote in Psalm 139.[22] David openly invited the Spirit of God to search him, to dig through his interior life and uncover any sin he found there. He even celebrated it. Confession is a terrifying gift, which sounds like a contradiction because it is.

The alternative to hiding is the refusal to hide. The terrifying insistence on exposing ourselves to God. That's the only way to open ourselves up to unconditional love. Ever wonder what made David a man after God's own heart? That's the phrase inscribed on his tombstone. But read his bio. He was also a liar, manipulator, adulterer (maybe rapist, depending on how you weigh the evidence), and a murderer! So what about his life made his heart like God's? Only this—the psalms he authored were peppered with personal confessions—honest, unfiltered, raw nakedness before God. He was a long way from perfection, but he refused to hide. When he realized he was naked, he didn't pick up fig leaves; he ran to the Father.

In the ancient Near Eastern world from which the Bible emerged, successive cultures built cities right on top of the ruins of old ones. People didn't bother developing new land. They just burned down what used to be there and built the new city right on top of the old. An archaeological dig in the Near East is discovering one period of history and then another period that is a layer beneath that, and then another. It's as though we need to wipe the dust off of story after story after story. That's confession—to excavate down into the layers of your own life, uncovering not just what's obvious on the surface but the layers of personal history underneath that continue to inform your present.

One of the biggest mistakes we've made in the modern church is to reimagine spiritual maturity as the need to confess less. The unspoken assumption is, "As I ascend in relationship with God, I confess less because I have less to confess." True spiritual maturity, though, is the opposite. It's not an ascension; it's an archaeological dig as we discover layer after layer of what was in us all along. Spiritual maturity means *more* confession, not less. Maturity is discovering the depths of my personal brand of fallenness and the depths to which God's grace has really penetrated, even without me knowing it.

The desperate need of our time is not for successful Christians, popular Christians, or winsome Christians; it's for deep Christians. And the only way to become a deep Christian is through the inner excavation called confession. The pathway of spiritual maturity is a descent, not an ascent. A maturing community is a confessing community—not a church without sin, but a church without secrets.

When we come in and out of God's presence in gathered communities with our deepest needs and secrets hidden, we are essentially saying, "Jesus' victory is not enough. It's not enough for me. Not enough for this. I just need more time. I can sort this out on my own." How do we combat the insistent, internal narrative that was planted in us at the fall, that keeps us in a perpetual state of hiding and dressing ourselves up with our choice fig leaves? Confession. We let David's words inspire our words. We take David's ancient prayers as the script for our current ones. You'll be hard-pressed to find a single one of his prayers that didn't involve undressing himself before God.

We say we believe in grace, but confession is how we actually trust what we already believe in. The very parts of our stories we most want to edit, or erase altogether, become the very parts of our stories we'd never take back and never stop telling. That's the kind of author God is.

Naked Revival

Count Nikolaus Ludwig von Zinzendorf (yes, that's his real name), a German twentysomething sitting on a sizable inheritance, turned the family property into a refugee relief camp in 1722. They gave the small Moravian village the name Herrnhut, meaning "the Lord's Watch." It was to become the birthplace of a great revival and the modern missions movement. It all began with a refugee village committing to 24-7 prayer, which, one hundred years of nonstop prayer later, became known as the Moravian revival (more on that later).

The really interesting bit of the story, though, is not the revival stories but the revival origins. If you read the direct accounts from those refugees, they don't make such a big deal about the prayer movement. The story they tell is about the unlikely night on which the prayer movement started.

Zinzendorf welcomed a group of refugees into the family of God and then gave them his radical vision—an early church kind of community alive again, here and now. The kind of community they intended to become required daily countercultural decisions to prioritize the other, and that's fundamentally against human nature. Naturally, five years in, there was widespread disillusionment, a whole lot of pain, a pervasive sense of disappointment, cynicism, blame, and plenty of settling for something just okay but far less than what they had envisioned together.

On August 13, 1727, they gathered for another ordinary church meeting. Zinzendorf preached a powerful sermon on the cross, and as he did, the Holy Spirit fell in such an overwhelming way that in that very moment, in that very meeting room, they began to confess their wrongs and forgive one another—no buts, no explanations, no holding back—just naming the wrongs and wiping the slate clean. The Spirit fell so heavily that they stayed for hours in confession and actually stumbled out of the church service dizzy with supernatural experience, like drunks out of a pub at last call.[23]

Two weeks after that night, they decided to start a prayer meeting. That prayer meeting lasted a hundred years. So how did the Moravian revival happen? Most historians say, "Prayer—the whole thing was fueled by prayer," and there's a lot of truth to that. But according to the forty-eight refugees in the room, the eyewitnesses who lived and experienced it, they would have said, "No, no, no. One hundred years of prayer was just the overflow of one night of unfiltered, healing confession."

Revival didn't happen because everyone agreed it was a good idea; it happened because everyone stripped off their fig leaves in front of one another.

Brennan Manning wrote, "Anyone God uses significantly is always deeply wounded . . . We are, each and every one of us, insignificant people whom God has called and graced to use in a significant way . . . On the last day, Jesus will look us over not for medals, diplomas, or honors, but for scars."[24] It is not by our gifts, insights, ideas, or qualifications that God is determined to heal the world, but by our scars. By his wounds we are healed,[25] and by our wounds the healing is shared.

Let the Bones You Have Crushed Rejoice

> Cleanse me with hyssop, and I will be clean;
>> wash me, and I will be whiter than snow.
> Let me hear joy and gladness;
>> let the bones you have crushed rejoice.
>
> Psalm 51:7–8

C. S. Lewis paints a vivid picture of the power of confession in *The Voyage of the Dawn Treader*. Eustace, a young boy who had traded his innocence to a deceiver when he didn't really know what he was doing, was forced to live in a covering of dragon skin in perpetuity, Lewis's mystical reimagining of Genesis's fig leaves. He'd tried to pull the dragon skin off himself plenty of times before, only to see it grow back again. Finally exhausted enough to simply lie still, Eustace is approached by the lion Aslan, who is terrifying but gentle—Lewis's depiction of Jesus.

> Then the lion said—but I don't know if it spoke—"You will have to let me undress you." I was afraid of his claws, I can tell you, but I was pretty nearly desperate now. So I just lay flat down on my back to let him do it.
>
> The very first tear he made was so deep that I thought it had gone right into my heart. And when he began pulling the skin off, it hurt worse than anything I've ever felt. The only thing

that made me able to bear it was just the pleasure of feeling the stuff peel off. You know—if you've ever picked the scab of a sore place. It hurts like billy-oh but it *is* such fun to see it coming away . . .

Well, he peeled the beastly stuff right off—just as I thought I'd done it myself the other three times, only they hadn't hurt—and there it was lying on the grass: only ever so much thicker, and darker, and more knobbly-looking than the others had been. And there was I as smooth and soft as a peeled switch and smaller than I had been. Then he caught hold of me—I didn't like that much for I was very tender underneath now that I'd no skin on—and threw me into the water. It smarted like anything but only for a moment. After that it became perfectly delicious and as soon as I started swimming and splashing I found that all the pain had gone from my arm. And then I saw why. I'd turned into a boy again.[26]

I want God's presence and power. I want to know in my days what Nikolaus von Zinzendorf knew in Herrnhut, what Paul knew in Ephesus, what Peter saw in Jerusalem. I hunger for God in my midst, the current experience of all that Jesus won for me. God's response to my desire is simple, loving, and straightforward: "You will have to let me undress you."

David knew what it felt like to be undressed and thrown into that water—the sting at first, and then the childlike joy of splashing around in the freedom and innocence of restored childlikeness. In Psalm 51, his famous confession, he used four different words to name his sin but nineteen different words to illustrate God's forgiveness. We have a limited number of ways to sin; his forgiveness, though, is limitless, infinite.[27]

"Let the bones you have crushed rejoice," shouts David. Let the place of soul-crushing agony, the secret I'm holding beneath the surface, the weight I'm lugging around, turn into pure joy—the dancing, laughing, shouting kind of joy.

"You will have to let me undress you."

PRACTICE

Searching and Naming

We begin by asking God to search us because he knows us even better than we know ourselves. We can trust him to gently, lovingly reveal ourselves to us, especially the parts we don't see, the ugly blemishes that may be obvious to others but hidden to us.

Once we've given space for self-examination, always in reliance on the Holy Spirit as the searching agent, we are ready to confess. Confession is as simple and unpretentious as it sounds. Whatever has been revealed to us, say it out loud to God. That's it. When we name it to God, we "bring it into the light,"[28] which weakens the power of sin and calls on the power of grace for healing and freedom. Much of the time, confession should be practiced in mature, trusted spiritual friendship, enabling the confessor to receive absolution in hearing the gospel preached back to them.

Most people go to the grave without ever confronting the false self—the deep patterns of dysfunction that govern their thoughts, feelings, and behaviors. Therefore, most people go to the grave never having felt the freedom of living as their true selves, never having given their true selves to the world and to those they love. To live apart from confession is an absolute tragedy, and to discover confession an unspeakable gift.

Confession is two parts: searching and naming. Searching is God's part; naming is ours.

Still your body and mind. Wait in silence, opening yourself up to the Spirit of God, releasing every possible interference. Then pray the words of David, restated as an invitation: "Search me, LORD, and know me." Wait. Pay attention to what may come up. Note how God begins to reveal you to yourself. Confess.

Chapter 5

ON EARTH AS IT
IS IN HEAVEN

Intercession

In that day you will no longer ask me anything.
Very truly I tell you, my Father will give you
whatever you ask in my name. Until now you
have not asked for anything in my name.

John 16:23–24

I was distracted by the buzz of Kirsten's phone against the lino-
leum table. It was Tuesday night, and I was sitting in a church
sanctuary in Queens, New York, filled with round tables, metal
folding chairs, and weak coffee in Styrofoam cups. The table around
which I sat was occupied by a few other pastors and their spouses,
taking some time to learn healthy communication from a wise older
couple who had done it well for decades.

This particular night, I can't tell you anything they said because
I was so distracted by the buzzing cell phone. Finally, Kirsten
picked it up and slipped out. It was Kurt, her father. He had been

desperately trying to reach us. "The doctor just left the room. Van isn't gonna make it." There was a lot more information, but his voice broke after that, choked back by a flood of emotion.

Kirsten's brother, Van, who also happens to be one of my closest friends (long story), had some chest pain he thought was heartburn a few days earlier. He'd had some spicy shrimp off a friend's grill, and he assumed it wasn't sitting quite right.

When he went to a walk-in clinic in search of an antacid, what he thought was heartburn turned out to be a torn aorta. His primary heart valve was gushing blood internally so fast they weren't sure he'd even make it to the hospital. While the doctor was explaining all this to Van—just in his early thirties—an ambulance was speeding, sirens blaring, to the clinic to pick him up.

Forty-eight hours later, the leading surgeon at Vanderbilt, America's top heart hospital by reputation, had just delivered the news: "He's not gonna make it. Tell the family to get here as quickly as they can."

We left the church right away. We rushed home and booked the next flight out. By the time we got to the hospital in Nashville the following morning, the medical team had more information. Van was scheduled for a surgery—a surgery that had a significantly greater chance of killing him than healing him. But he was dying, and this was quite literally the only option left.

I sat on the armrest of the chair at the foot of his bed and dropped my head into my hands, peering through my fingers at Van's tattooed chest. They would slice his skin down the middle and peel open his rib cage in the next twenty-four hours. I was there to say goodbye to someone I was supposed to grow old next to. I brought all the crushing desperation and fear, all the measly hope I could muster, and talked to God about it. I prayed.

That was the beginning of the story. Here's how it ended: a couple days later, Van woke up in that same hospital room after a successful surgery, the only patient in the hospital's history to survive this particular combination of multiple open-heart surgeries.

The leading surgeon came in to speak to the family. He wept as he recounted the moment in the operating room when the surgical team gave up and informally declared Van deceased. Then a nursing student, whose only role was to hand the surgeon the scissors, began praying for him in the operating room. Immediately, the surgeon located the bleeding tear he had been unsuccessfully searching for over the last five hours, and Van survived.

Miraculous. That's not my word. That's what the non-Christian, non-praying doctor called it as he relayed the story, with tears threatening to overflow the banks of his eyelids.

Yes, prayer stills us, brings us peace, helps us come to terms with what is. Prayer changes the person praying from the inside out. But prayer also releases power. Prayer releases power to affect real change in the tangible world.

Monica's Son

Monica was a single mom with one child, a son. She was a devout believer who sang hymns over her child in his infancy and prayed nightly with her hand on his forehead.

The boy grew up to see the world quite differently from his mother. As an adolescent, he became known in their North African town as a womanizer and would often be seen publicly drunk at untold hours of the night. He had an extraordinary intellect and eventually grew into a philosopher, channeling all of his energy into combatting his mother's Christian faith.

Monica didn't give up. She continued to pray nightly for her son's salvation, just as she had done with her hand on his tiny forehead when she was a young mother. When he was nineteen, she had a dream through which she believed God was promising to answer her prayers for her son.

In response to her dream, she grew more intense in her prayer. A year passed, then another year, then another. There was no change. No moment of hope. No change of heart or openness to belief.

Nine years after that dream, he made plans to travel to Rome, known for its revelry and debauchery. Monica stayed awake all night in intense prayer that God would prevent his travels. Little did she know that her son had changed his plans and sailed for Rome that very night, already on his way as she prayed.

On that trip, sitting alone one afternoon in a Roman garden, Monica's son heard the audible voice of God speaking to him. Bewildered, he opened up the very Scriptures he had dedicated himself to despising and disproving. Right then and there, he surrendered his life to Jesus.

Monica's son's name was Augustine, and he went on to be widely considered the greatest theologian in history and a father to the early Christian church. Prayer releases power.

Paralyzed between Wonder and Mystery

Prayer is a compelling wonder. God acting on earth in response to conversation with a human being? How can it be? How can there be a God this powerful and yet this personal? It's better than we dare to imagine most of the time. Walter Wink confidently exclaims, "History belongs to the intercessors, who believe the future into being."[1]

And prayer is also a confounding mystery. Some readers will be inspired and motivated by those stories of answered prayer, but at least as many will be confused, or even angered, by the same stories.

"That's great that your brother-in-law was healed, but why some and not others? What about all the similar prayers that went unanswered? If we insist on celebrating divine action, can someone please explain divine silence?"

"I'm truly happy for Augustine and his mom—I really am. But what took God so long? Why wait decades to answer a prayer, and then answer it? Is there some kind of divine equation with just the right combination of time spent praying plus number of people praying plus method of praying that finally gets God's attention? Or is God just unmotivated most of the time, and she finally caught God at the right moment? And in what other context does withholding that kind of power for years make sense? Doesn't that story speak more of the cruelty of a God with the power to act who carries out that action slowly, apathetically, and randomly more than it does to the kindness of a God who acts in response to prayer?"

The question we're circling around is this: "Do my prayers matter in any visible, tangible sense? Is God carrying on the way he would always carry on, regardless of whether or not I pray? Do my requests exclusively reform my heart in some divine equation, or do they carry the power to change real people, conditions, and circumstances in the world I inhabit? Do my prayers actually matter?"

C. S. Lewis set up the case against prayer by mimicking the voice of a skeptic: "Even if I grant your point and admit that answers to prayer are theoretically possible, I still think they are infinitely improbable. I don't think it at all likely that God requires the ill-informed (and contradictory) advice of us humans as to how to run the world. If He is all-wise, as you say He is, doesn't He know already what is best? And if He is all-good, won't He do it whether we pray or not?"[2]

For however many of us who celebrate with the fiery faithful that "history belongs to the intercessors," at least as many of us just shrug our shoulders with the skeptic. Here is where our prayers live—paralyzed between wonder and mystery.

"History belongs to the intercessors"—what a compelling wonder! That is, until we actually begin to pray, and all that confidence and inspiration are drowned in a tsunami of questions, doubts, confusion, and past disappointment.

Don't get me wrong, plenty of us keep on praying in that paralyzing space between wonder and mystery, but we don't pray in the way of Jesus. Our prayers don't reflect the wide-eyed, blazing sense of empowerment that the Son of Man's words engender in anyone who really believes them. We pray the safest kind of prayers—the ones so passive and vague we'd never be able to tell if God responded to them or not.

As a thought experiment, try to recall everything you've prayed for in the last week. If God answered every last one of your prayers, what would happen? With the exception of one or two particularly bold or naive people, the answer is usually very little. This place between wonder and mystery paralyzes us.

Jesus' disciples said to him, "Teach us to pray."[3]

He responded, "This, then, is how you should pray: 'Our Father in heaven . . .'"[4]

Most love the opening line. Beautiful! One God and Father to the whole world.

"Hallowed be your name . . ."[5]

Ugh. We're a bit more resistant to that part. It makes God seem like a bit of a narcissist, but I guess if there is a Creator that powerful and that loving, he has earned some hallowing. So, we can get there.

"Your kingdom come, your will be done, on earth as it is in heaven."[6]

That's where he loses us.

Prayer as a way to meditate and let go? Definitely.

Prayer as a centering exercise? Essential.

Prayer as a channel to be reformed from the inside out? Of course.

Prayer that really works? The sort of prayer that joins God to bring about redemption and push back the darkness? Prayer that actually makes a marked difference in the visible, tangible world, in the lives of the real people I interact with and in the real issues they face? The sort of prayer that brings heaven to earth? Here is where opinions splinter in every direction. This is where he loses us.

To Jesus' credit, he did everything he could to make sure he didn't lose us here. He never backed down or qualified his statement. In fact, he kept saying this kind of thing. Here's a sampling of what Jesus had to say on the subject of prayer:

> Ask and it will be given to you; seek and you will find; knock and the door will be opened to you. (Luke 11:9)

> Therefore I tell you, whatever you ask for in prayer, believe that you have received it, and it will be yours. (Mark 11:24)

> And I will do whatever you ask in my name, so that the Father may be glorified in the Son. You may ask me for anything in my name, and I will do it. (John 14:13–14)

> If you remain in me and my words remain in you, ask whatever you wish, and it will be done for you. (John 15:7)

> If you believe, you will receive whatever you ask for in prayer. (Matthew 21:22)

If you, then, though you are evil, know how to give good gifts to your children, how much more will your Father in heaven give good gifts to those who ask him! (Matthew 7:11)

If we really took Jesus' invitation seriously, if we really believed in the sort of prayer that Jesus talked about, the modern church would have a hard time getting its people to do anything *but* pray. In actuality, we need to be motivated *to* pray. And that's because most people, even the most serious, mature Christians, don't buy prayer as Jesus described it, not entirely anyway.

It is absolutely true that prayer is equal parts wonder and mystery, but more than anything else, prayer is a profound invitation. Prayer is, I believe, the most profound invitation God offers us on the other side of grace. And this invitation is not just for the pious or the lucky; it's for all of us.

The "on earth as it is in heaven" kind of praying is technically called "intercessory prayer." Biblically, our English word *intercession* comes from the Old Testament Hebrew word *paga'*, and in New Testament Greek, it's *enteuxis*. The English word is derived from the Latin word *intercedo*, meaning "to come between."[7] In both ancient and modern expressions, to intercede means to go between, to intervene between two parties, to mediate. In lay terms, intercessory prayer simply means to pray for someone else.

The motive behind all true intercessory prayer is love for the other. Jesus isn't describing some real-life version of wishes to a cosmic genie that occasionally come true if you figure out the formula. He's talking about the kind of prayers that start with love for someone else and end with inviting God's activity into places where that love is lacking. Intercession is a willing and intentional choice to turn from the endless spiral into the self—my desires, my needs, my circumstances—to the desires, needs, and circumstances of another. To utter even a syllable of intercessory prayer is a profound act of love.

Richard Foster writes, "If we truly love people, we will desire for them far more than it is within our power to give them, and this will lead us to prayer. Intercession is a way of loving others . . . Intercessory Prayer is selfless prayer, even self-giving prayer. In the ongoing work of the kingdom of God, nothing is more important than Intercessory Prayer."[8]

God's Original Plan

To see the invitation, to begin to regain movement from the paralyzed spot we've all gotten stuck in, we need to start all the way back at the beginning. The story of prayer, as laid out in Scripture, can be summarized in four episodes (or eras): creation, fall, promise, and Jesus.

Creation: The Life God Intended

All the way back on the Bible's opening page, at the beginning of the world, God created "Adam," which in Hebrew means "person" or "human." Where you and I read "man" or "mankind" in the English translation of Genesis, we are reading the same Hebrew word translated as the personal name "Adam" elsewhere in the narrative. In fact, the Hebrew word is *adam*, spelled exactly like it's spelled in English.

The claim found on page 1 of the Bible, bound up in the first name of history's first man is this: This isn't just a story of God and one guy named Adam; this is the story of God and all of us. It's every individual's story.

The great existential question that has plagued every philosopher all the way back through recorded history goes something like this: "Why are we here?" To state it theistically, "Why were we created?" Genesis offers a surprisingly direct answer to that weighty question:

> Then God said, "Let us make mankind in our image, in our likeness, so that they may rule over the fish in the sea and the birds in the sky, over the livestock and all the wild animals, and over all the creatures that move along the ground." (Genesis 1:26)

Why were you created? The biblical answer is "to rule." And this is not a manipulative, power-hungry sort of "rule." It's an *imago dei* (image of God) kind of authority, ruling on earth as a direct reflection of God's Trinitarian character. Human beings were made to be intercessors participating with God in lovingly overseeing the world, set apart, bearing God's authority to rule in selfless love.

In Hebrew, the same language used in Genesis 1 for *rule* was ascribed to kings and queens. Ruling is a royal task. Rabbi Lord Jonathan Sacks summarizes: "We know that in the ancient world it was rulers, emperors and pharaohs who were held to be in the image of God. So what Genesis was saying was that we are all royalty."[9]

God made Adam and Eve his managers here on the earth—God's intercessors entrusted to call the shots. Psalm 115 puts it bluntly: "The highest heavens belong to the LORD, but the earth he has given to mankind."[10] It's important to understand the meaning of this "given" earth. God did not completely forfeit the earth to people, dust off his divine hands, and get on with the next project. He maintained *and maintains* sovereignty and ultimate governing authority over the activities of his own creation. But God did *and does* share the responsibility of managing the earth with people. Or to say it biblically, God made us to be his intercessors.

God created you and me in his image and gave us a creation

to manage. This place we inhabit is our assignment—to spread his image into every square inch.

Fall: The Life We Actually Live

Anyone thoughtfully reading the Genesis origin story should immediately be asking the obvious question, "Where did it all go wrong?" If God's plan is for people to rule over his creation as his image bearers, we are doing a subpar job, and that's putting it politely.

The environment is falling apart to such a degree that scientists are predicting end dates on an earth that can support human life. Natural resources are being pillaged from the nations where they're most needed and overconsumed by those who have plenty. Half of the world is dying of starvation, while the other half dies of obesity. So the obvious question to anyone dog-earing the page at the end of Genesis 2 is, "Where did God's intention for creation go so horribly wrong?"

Scripture makes the claim that all this dysfunction is the result of a deception. You and I lost who we are. We forfeited our role as God's intercessors, co-managers of his creation.

The story is a familiar one. Satan tempts Adam and Eve. They believe his deception. They act on that deception. Pain and suffering enter our world. And with that, the line of communication between God and people is fractured.

The Genesis conflict is threefold: (1) You have a spiritual enemy; (2) the weapon of that enemy is deception; and (3) the effect of that deception is paralysis. The authority to rule God's creation, given to you and me in Genesis 2, was usurped by Satan in Genesis 3.

Russell, an effortlessly cool friend of mine with an eye for beauty, was on vacation outside of Nashville. He got up before the sun one morning, hopped on his motorbike, and took a winding rural road en route to a picturesque spot he had scouted out. His plan was to set up his camera and catch the sunrise on time lapse— documenting the early-morning wonder of that great ball of fire peeking over the horizon.

Another driver found him later that morning. His motorbike was lying on its side just off the road and his body was splayed out several yards away, breathing but unresponsive. A helicopter rushed him to the hospital in what seemed to be a futile attempt to save his life. Miraculously, days later, despite every medical reason to give up hope, his eyes opened. He was alive, but he had sustained a severe brain injury.

For months afterward, Russell lived in a rehab facility where he worked on retraining the damaged part of his brain, which was connected to his motor skills. His brain activity was working fine, but you couldn't tell that by looking at him. The simplest everyday unconscious thought would pass through his mind—something like, *Move your right hand.* But his hand didn't respond. It stayed there, glued to his thigh.

The damage, put in terms I could understand, was "there was a communication breach somewhere between Russell's head and his hand." He still had all the intellectual capacity of a gifted, highly creative professional in his late twenties, but on my first visit to see him, the attending nurse fed him ice chips by hand. There was a break in the communication line between his mind and his body.

I can still see the look on Russell's face from my first visit to see him. As the nurse's latex-gloved hand slipped a chip of ice between his teeth, he was staring at me, eyes wide, almost with terror. Russell was trapped inside a body that didn't work. He could see and think and desire, but his action was paralyzed. All the power was still there, but the line of communication between intention and action was broken. I sat there staring back at him just as intently, though instead of terror, my eyes were filling with tears.

I wanted so badly to free him, but this was a lock I couldn't pick. The imprisonment was inside him.

That's something like the condition we're left in after Genesis 3. We are trapped in a communication breach. God created an inseparable connection between his mind and our action. We are Christ's body on earth,[11] but the line of communication was broken in the fall.

We look around the world and see the dysfunction surrounding us everywhere—suffering, pain, injustice, oppression—but we lack the capacity to set the world right, to "rule," to use the language of Genesis. Because somewhere between God's mind and our action, the signals are cut off. The imprisonment is inside us. We carry the image and authority of a perfect, loving God. It's all still there. But we are paralyzed by a communication breach.

Promise: The Living Victory

The prophet Isaiah foretold the birth of a coming Messiah: "For to us a child is born, to us a son is given, and the government will be on his shoulders."[12] God is coming to earth as one of us. The author is writing himself into the story in the person of Jesus. "To us a child is born!" That line's a showstopper on Christmas Eve by candlelight, but it's a whole lot more than that. "The government will be on his shoulders." That's a political statement. It's authority language. It's about rule. A fitting restatement of Isaiah's promise would be, "He's coming to win back the role we lost, to repair the communication breach."

Fulfilling Isaiah's prophecy, Jesus said, "Now is the judgment of this world; now will the ruler of this world be cast out."[13]

Why were you and I created? To rule.

What does Jesus call Satan? Ruler. Genesis language.

What does Jesus promise? To win our rule back. The Genesis promise.

At the close of the Gospels, after Jesus' life, death, and resurrection, he sums up his victory in the famous words, *"All authority* in heaven and on earth has been *given to me."*[14] God won our authority back. He restored the very position for which you and I were created. He stepped into the tension we feel all the time and cut a way through. He made us intercessors again.

Jesus: The Restoration of Prayer

On the final night of Jesus' life, in a candid moment with his disciples, the apostle John records arguably the most empowering and confusing words Jesus ever said: "Very truly I tell you, it is for your good that I am going away. Unless I go away, the Advocate will not come to you; but if I go, I will send him to you."[15]

It reads like a sitcom breakup speech. Jesus is saying, with a straight face, "It's better for you if I go. I'm no good for you. It's not you; it's me." He's telling them that, very soon, as Alan Jones puts it, "he is going to leave them, and this time for good (in both senses of the word)."[16]

It may read like a breakup speech, but it's the furthest thing from it. Jesus is talking about prayer. In the same breath, he goes on to explain, "In that day you will no longer ask me anything. Very truly I tell you, my Father will give you whatever you ask in my name. Until now you have not asked for anything in my name."[17]

Jesus is unmistakably explaining, "You've gotten used to bringing requests, needs, questions, and complaints to me in person, but soon you'll go directly to the Father, just as you've seen me do." He's talking about prayer.

Prayer is the pathway God has made to get us back to his original plan. Prayer is the way we can rule, manage, intercede for this world. Prayer is the repair of the communication breach that paralyzes us. Philip Yancey says, "Of all the means God could have used, prayer seems the weakest, slipperiest, and easiest to ignore. So it is, unless Jesus was right in that most baffling claim. He went away for our sakes, as a form of power sharing, to invite us into direct communion with God and to give us a crucial role in the struggle against the forces of evil."[18] God has shared his power with you. He calls you a co-manager of heaven, walking around on earth. Prayer is how this moves from a biblical rumor to your actual, everyday experience.

Jesus is very plainly telling his disciples, "Until now, you've never really prayed, not like I designed it. But when I go to the Father, you'll discover prayer in my name." The ancient phrase "in my name" means "under my authority." To pray in Jesus' name means to pray with recovered authority. He won back on our behalf the authority we were created to carry and lost. "In Jesus' name" was never meant to become just a fitting tagline at the end of the prayers of experienced Christians. It's the exercise of Jesus' victory. To pray is to experience the very same access to God the Father that Jesus has.

New Testament scholar Larry Hurtado writes, "To pray in Jesus' name . . . means that we enter into Jesus' status in God's favour, and invoke Jesus' standing with God."[19]

You're not Jesus. But if you're a follower of Jesus, every single time you pray, you come before the Father clothed in the robe and crown of a ruler. In the eyes of heaven, you are filled with Jesus' status and standing.

When God won your authority back, God was winning prayer back.

Sharing Heaven

The Swiss theologian Karl Barth once said, "To clasp the hands in prayer is the beginning of an uprising against the disorder of the world."[20] Prayer is the means by which we push back the curse that's infected the world and infected us.

When we engage in intercessory prayer, we are loving others on the basis of heaven's resources. Prayer is heaven's highest security clearance—free access to stroll right into the heavenly vault, gather up whatever we can carry, and hand it out to the world. We are rulers, calling the shots for how heavenly resources are distributed, and intercession is a way of saying, "Oh, we've gotta have some here. Look, there's something missing over there." It is the distribution of God's resources in the familiar environments that comprise our disordered world—among coworkers, roommates, neighbors, and strangers; at bars, cafés, and soup kitchens; at high-rises, housing projects, homeless shelters, and prisons. P. T. Forsyth writes, "Prayer has its great end when it lifts us to be conscious and more sure of the gift than the need, of the grace than the sin."[21]

Intercessory prayer simultaneously restores our world and restores the God-given identity that was breathed into us first. It is the active experience of restoring creation.

The Church's Worst-Kept Secret

All that being true, and it absolutely is, the worst-kept secret in church history is that most people, even most Christians, don't really like prayer. Don't get me wrong, we still do it, mainly out of guilt or obligation or because we know it's good for us, making prayer the spiritual equivalent of eating celery.

But what if, according to Jesus, you've never really prayed? "Until now you have not asked for anything in my name."[22] What if you've never come before the Father, wearing the robes of the heir, carrying the standing and status of Jesus? What if you've never plundered the riches stored away in the heavenly vault? What if you've never pushed back the curse alongside God? It's already been defeated. He's just looking for intercessors to implement the already-secured victory.

"Hold on, that's prayer? Well, I could wake up a few minutes earlier for that. I'd spend my lunch hour differently for that. I might even skip a meal or two for that."

Here's the best part of the whole story, the bit that really blows my mind. God doesn't need intercessors managing his creation. He's not overwhelmed by all the responsibility of overseeing the world. He's all-knowing, all-powerful, and completely outside of time. He's got this. God doesn't need intercessors; God chooses intercessors.

We dream of a God who brings heaven to earth; God dreams of praying people to share heaven with.

Again, I'll pose the simplest question: If God gave you everything you've prayed for in the last week, what would happen?

The only reason I ask is that you are a ruler, a co-heir with Christ, a manager of heavenly resources. What are you doing with all that authority? If we really took Jesus seriously on the invitation to prayer, what would happen? What would happen in you? What would happen to your community? What would happen in your city? Isn't it worth finding out?

Becoming Our Prayers

I sat next to Diego on the bus stop bench, his suitcase between us. He was dead set on running away, offering a murky plan of how he'd get from the Port Authority Bus Terminal in Times Square all the way to San Juan, Puerto Rico, where his sister lived, on nothing but the change in his pocket. It was a flimsy plan at best. He had called me to come and say goodbye, but I suspected he was actually inviting me just so somebody sensible would talk him out of this.

I met Diego a few years prior, as a sixteen-year-old who was entering the ninth grade. He had been held back at that point and was on a fast track to dropping out altogether. He had entered high school at just a third-grade reading level. I was introduced to him by his teacher, who attended my church community and suggested Diego could use a male role model.

He grew up in the housing projects on Avenue D, the most dangerous block in New York City's infamous Alphabet City. Given where he came from, Diego was remarkably well-adjusted. He avoided trouble, kept good attendance at school, and was a generally happy kid. That is, until his father was arrested for possession and distribution of narcotics.

Diego was at home for the police raid. He watched them cuff his dad's hands behind his back and read him his Miranda rights. In the weeks that followed, it was discovered that he was both dealing drugs out of their apartment and keeping Diego's mother well supplied, resulting in what appeared to be irreparable damage to her mind and emotions.

It was only a few months after the arrest that Diego's teacher introduced us. By now he was drinking heavily and applying himself much less at school. I had no idea how to help him. What chance did he have? What did it mean for him to follow Jesus, for the kingdom to come—in his family, his home, his life here on earth—as it is in heaven?

Pete Greig writes, "Intercession is impossible until we allow the things that break God's heart to break our hearts as well."[23] I hadn't the first idea how to help this kid, but his story broke my heart, and that led me to prayer. I awoke daily before sunrise to walk a two-mile route along Avenue D that ended at Diego's building. On those walks, I prayed the Lord's Prayer thematically, each line serving as inspiration for personal dialogue, always lingering longest on the phrase "your kingdom come, your will be done, on earth as it is in heaven." I prayed that phrase particularly over Diego as I neared his home, walking right past the bus stop bench where we sat on this particular night.

Matthew's record of Jesus' "Lord's Prayer" is broken into two sets of three petitions, turning on the hinge phrase "on earth as it is in heaven" right in the center, holding the prayer together like binding to a book. The first half of the prayer gets us into God's reality. "The first three petitions make us participants in the being and action of God," notes Eugene Peterson.[24] The pronouns tell the story—your name, your kingdom, your will. Your, your, your. The three concluding prepositions invite God to return the favor—to get his heavenly reality into us while our feet remain planted here on the ground. There's an obvious shift in the pronouns. Give us, forgive us, lead us. Us, us, us. Peterson continues, "Prayer involves us deeply and responsibly in all the operations of God. Prayer also involves God deeply and transformatively in all the details of our lives."[25]

I had no idea that God would employ me in answer to my own prayers, but that's how intercession often works. Sometimes God will move heaven and earth, bending space and time to weave a supernatural narrative in response to our prayers. But God *always* purposes prayer to change the heart of the intercessor themselves. Profound answers to prayer come equally in the forms of God's independent action and God's partnering action to reform and work through the praying person. Intercessory prayer is often about what the intercessor has become after they're finished praying.

Prayer. That's how I ended up at this bus stop in the middle of the night. Somewhere in the midst of all those mornings in prayer, a bit of Jesus' long-suffering love for Diego had gotten into me, so when he called that night, I knew there was nowhere else I'd rather be.

Sometime around 1:00 a.m., after watching a few buses roll past, I talked Diego into sleeping on it before making a final decision. A year later, I was driving him three hundred miles north with every trinket he owned packed into my car. He had enrolled in a small state university right along the Canadian border. Diego not only graduated from high school, but he became student body president during his senior year. He was the first in his family to enroll in and later graduate from college.

Of course, Diego's story is one of many, and not all of them have fairy-tale endings. In fact, his story is still very much in the middle of the plot, an ongoing story, but his is a real story, not a fairy tale. And his is a story in which I have found myself a privileged and unlikely participant. And the theme behind it all? Intercession.

Intercession is nothing more than ordinary love combined with sober humility. I love Diego, and his needs exceed my capacity, so what fills the space between love and humility? Prayer. The powerful prayers of intercession. And those who dare to pray and keep praying get to live the adventures that run parallel to the unseen, hidden labor of prayer.

A House of Prayer in Brooklyn

In the winter of 2019, after ringing in the New Year by walking prayer circles around the holy ground known as my public middle school, I was back in Brooklyn (my home at the time), leading a church of ordinary radicals crazy enough to take Jesus' prayer invitation seriously and personally.

We met in a converted Jewish synagogue. Save for a rickety set of stairs in the back corner, it was just an open room with a stage at the front and stacks of flimsy Ikea chairs set out on Sunday mornings. The creaky stairs climbed up to what, in some ancient past, was a small balcony. We had converted it into two rooms, both about eight by ten feet. One was the shared office for our modest staff; the other became a nursery where we crammed way too many babies into a tiny room with a few brave volunteers every Sunday. The other six days of the week, it sat empty.

A few of us started dreaming. What if we were to dedicate that little room to prayer?

We covered the walls in craft paper, the sort a proper butcher wraps around cuts of meat. In one corner, we stationed an old church kneeler, pockets worn in the wood where so many knees had sunk. A Bible sat atop it, in this place where the sweeping promises of God would be turned into whispered, personal prayers. Another corner housed a water basin and a hand towel. Picture frames held verses of pardon for sin above it, a place to confess and be restored, washed, made clean. A cross leaned against the wall, with heavy nails on the floor at its base, a meditation on the cost of restoring this divine communication breach. On a table by the door rested a gold plate that held a few broken crackers and a glass of wine—a place to taste the story of grace, forgiveness, redemption, and restoration on our tongues. A sign hung outside the nursery door: "Please remove your shoes. The place you are entering is holy ground." It was both honest and comical. Our "holy ground" still held the stench of dirty diapers from the previous Sunday. It was ordinary ground, there was no disguising that. But it was becoming holy with each person who slipped off their shoes and walked in, filling the silence of that room with words of prayer.

We drew on the 24-7 prayer movement as inspiration—a rambunctious collection of communities from across the globe that was nearing twenty years of unceasing prayer at the time.[26] We divided six days of the week into one-hour time slots and invited people to sign up (on Sundays it served as a nursery). A leader from the movement kindly advised me, "If you don't get the first two weeks filled before you announce it to the congregation, you don't stand a chance." We knew there would be initial excitement, but it would taper off. Our appetite for the *idea* of prayer tends to be stronger than our stomach for the *actual experience* of prayer, unfortunately.

I begged and pleaded with our staff, our leaders, and our most committed congregants to sign up for at least one hour before we made the mid-January announcement. We nearly got those two weeks full. Not quite, but we were close. Most of us had never clicked our phones off, closed the door to a room, and talked to God for a full, uninterrupted hour before.

I signed up for the first hour, early on a Friday morning. When I walked out an hour later, I had scribbled a single prayer on the wall; other than that it was untouched. I took an Uber straight to the airport to catch a flight.

When I returned to Brooklyn a week later, I slipped in for another hour. I staggered—that's not hyperbole, I actually staggered—upon entrance. It was a mess. A beautiful mess. The walls were covered in prayers. They looked like the bare back of a tattoo enthusiast. Words, pictures, and Scriptures overlapping each other. Honest words, the kind you never hear in a church small group, spilled out of hearts onto the wall, awaiting a God who responds. Names of lost friends and family members stretched the full length of the room, just above the baseboard. Prayer for salvation awaiting the Good Shepherd, who leaves the ninety-nine for the one lost sheep. There were drawings elegant enough to make Monet blush, gritty enough to make Banksy jealous, and childlike enough it could've been a toddler's hand doing the sketch—all of them masterpieces in the eye of the only One in the audience. There were confessions, longings, hopes, and fears. I was surrounded by the deepest cries of the community I love, all of them held out vulnerably, awaiting an answer. We were finally in a position to be dazzled or disappointed by God, but nothing in-between. The goalie had been pulled, the harness removed, the safety activated.

"Alright, God. This is what you've been waiting for, right?" That's what I prayed with a quake in my voice. Then I fell to my knees in the middle of that tiny room, undone by the beauty of it all.

After two weeks, the prayer hours we feared would sit empty were already completely booked for the duration of that month of unceasing prayer. No one lost their appetite for the ordinary experience of prayer. In fact, many discovered they had a yearning appetite for more.

If we really took Jesus seriously on the invitation to prayer, what would happen? What would happen in you? What would happen to your community? What would happen in your city? We decided to find out.

PRACTICE

On Earth as It Is in Heaven

"Your kingdom come, your will be done, on earth as it is in heaven."

This is how Jesus teaches us to intercede. There are two movements to intercession: releasing and asking.

Your will be done. This part of the prayer is about releasing control. Think of something in your life you're wrestling for control over. Name one thing you've never released to God, or perhaps released in the past but are trying to grab back. When you've come up with it, name it and release it. Ask for filling from the Spirit in place of releasing, peace in place of anxiety, trust in place of fear, and so on.

Posture can be helpful in this act of prayer. As you open your hands, picture in your hands some part of your life, something you're clenching tightly to and trying to force your own will on. When you are ready, flip over your hands, physically symbolizing letting go, releasing control to God, setting those circumstances at the feet of Jesus. Turn your hands upward once again, this time open to receive the fruit of the Spirit in place of what you just released.

Your kingdom come . . . on earth as it is in heaven. Having released control and surrendered our own will, we are now free to see our lives, our relationships, our community, and our world through the eyes of God. It is from this place that we ask with hearts full of faith and hope.

Simply and clearly ask that God's kingdom will come where it is absent—friends outside of a relationship with Jesus, needs in our city and world, troubling or challenging circumstances, physical or mental illnesses. Ask for Jesus to come—anywhere and everywhere you know God's kingdom of love and peace is lacking.

In your asking, be brief and be specific. We tend to pray wordy, vague prayers when asking, almost like we're afraid to lay our requests before him boldly. Resist the urge to cover for God or make it easy on him. He can handle your requests. Just ask.

Chapter 6

DAILY BREAD

Petition

We circled the parking lot for a second time. I was sitting in the back seat of my mother-in-law's SUV in a well-to-do suburb a couple days after Christmas. The sprawling shopping center was dotted with chain restaurants and chain stores, and we weren't the only ones needing to make a quick return or two from our Christmas morning gift exchange. She slowly circled, waiting to pounce on any vacant patch of concrete the instant someone's reverse lights clicked on.

That's when I heard her say it to no one in particular. Well, technically it was to someone in particular. She addressed the statement very personally, but it rolled off her tongue like an afterthought. "Jesus, help us find a parking spot."

Are you kidding me? I thought to myself from the back seat.

We are operating an unnecessarily large vehicle for reasons I assume are aesthetic, despite the well-known fact that vehicles of this size overconsume limited natural resources, and you've got the audacity to plead help from the God who created this world we're so thoughtlessly plundering?

We are waiting approximately 120 additional seconds to walk inside to exchange a few garments we don't need anyway. And you're gonna ask the God whose arrival provoked the command that "anyone who has two shirts should share with the one who has none"[1] to help you pick out something more tasteful for our overstuffed closets?

With a straight face, you're gonna ask God to bend the arc of the universe in the direction of your shopping convenience when 690 million people are going hungry today,[2] and we're probably gonna let the leftovers in our overflowing holiday fridge go bad? Don't you think God is too busy addressing the hunger pangs of those people to worry about our wait to get into the shopping mall?

My internal monologue (thank God I didn't say any of that out loud) was interrupted by her voice. "Yes! There's one. Thank you, Jesus!"

This story is mostly hyperbole. All the facts are true, but I'm not quite that unbearably judgmental. Close, but not quite that bad.

This is where so many of us get hung up when it comes to prayer—the asking part. Jesus insists on it though. Jesus insists on "world hunger" prayers and "parking space" prayers alike. He won't have it any other way. Right in the middle of a prayer as cosmic as "hallowed be your name," as apocalyptic as "your kingdom come," as contrite as "forgive us," and as spiritual as "deliver us from the evil one," Jesus includes the unavoidably practical, circumstantial, and immediate "give us today our daily bread."[3]

Prayer, at its simplest and most straightforward, is asking God for help. But what are the guidelines to the "help" we can and should ask for? Surely there are some sincere requests selfish enough or impractical enough that God just laughs them off. Where does my will stop and God's begin? How do I ask in a way that's in line with God's eternal perspective? What's worth praying about, and what's just life? And at the end of the day, does Jesus really care about parking spaces?

Gratitude

The hinge point of Jesus' instructive, exemplary prayer is the phrase "on earth as it is in heaven." Two claims are hidden in this turn of phrase. The first is that heaven is the engine room for our prayers. Everything we can think to ask for finds its source in heaven. The second claim is that earth, the very ground we stand on while uttering our requests, is where the action happens. Heaven is the engine room, but earth is where our prayers are answered, are made visible. Earth is the atmosphere that heaven invades in response to our requests.

When Jesus illustrates prayer for the disciples and crowd of hangers-on, he tells the story of a neighbor needing—wait for it—bread. It's real language, earthy language, honest, everyday language. Daily bread language.

Christians today tend to fill their prayers with euphemisms and phrases only heard between "Dear God" and "Amen." At some point, the church invented a prayer language, which has been passed on to many of us. Jesus teaches a way of prayer that invites the common language we hear at the deli counter, on the street corners, in business meetings, and over drinks with friends.

When the language we use in our prayers stays grounded, our prayers tend to stay grounded too. Ordinary language keeps us from lofty prayers that usher the activity of God into some far-off imaginative place and instead invites God into the here and now, into the concerns of today—what I'll eat, who I'll meet, what I'll do, and how I'll feel about it all along the way. "On *earth* as it is in heaven" prayers. Daily bread prayers.

Jesus unmistakably rips prayer out of the sacred, stained-glassed, ornate walls of the church and places it in the commonness of everyday life. Prayer is not the ascent of the soul to some other place; it deals directly with our basic day-to-day needs and wants. Prayer is about the demands, obligations, and privileges of this very day.

If we pray for an end to global hunger but neglect to "say grace" over the pineapple fried rice we picked up for tonight's dinner, we miss out on a lot. If we pray for environmental sustainability but fail to whisper thanksgiving at the summit of a Saturday afternoon hike, our God is smaller for our trouble, not larger. If we pray for justice in the fashion industry's East Asian factories but ignore the person ringing up our Christmas exchange as they work a holiday double shift at H&M to make ends meet, we're missing the forest for the trees. And if we effortlessly judge the parking space prayers of someone else, sure that we know the priorities of an incomprehensible God, our spiritual lives are suffocating and restricted while their God is ever involved, interested, present.

If we pray for only big things, exclusively limiting our conversation with God to the objectively noble requests, we live a cramped spiritual life, with little room for the actual God we meet in Jesus.

Gratitude is the God-given reward for those who can stomach praying for small things.[4]

As my mother-in-law pulled into that parking space, there was gratitude in her heart and bitterness in mine. Peruvian philosopher and father of liberation theology Gustavo Gutiérrez says the basic diet of the healthy soul consists of prayer, justice, and gratitude.[5] It's possible (though I think quite unlikely) that I had a proper view of justice and a considerable point about prayer in the back-and-forth volley of my own internal monologue, but my soul was shriveled and weak from a lack of gratitude, while my mother-in-law's was healthy and expansive.

Ronald Rolheiser, professor at the Oblate School of Theology, bluntly states, "To be a saint is to be fueled by gratitude, nothing more and nothing less . . . Only one kind of person transforms the world spiritually, someone with a grateful heart."[6]

When you picture the face of God, what expression does he wear? Is the God of your imagination stern, serious, determined, even angry? Or maybe your vision of God is one in which he is aloof, uninterested, apathetic? The manner in which you answer that question will tell you a lot about your own spirituality. Julian of Norwich, a thirteenth-century English anchoress, described God as "completely relaxed and courteous, he [God] was himself the happiness and peace of his dear friends, his beautiful face radiating measureless love like a marvellous symphony."[7] She imagined God grateful and at peace in the company of friends, content to love them, his love radiating from his face in a supernatural smile.

There is a pathway to gratitude hidden in prayer—in our daily bread. Ask and keep asking. Ask for big and small things. "Kingdom come" and grace before supper. When we pray the Jesus way, keeping our prayers as common as our everyday small talk, we put one foot in front of the other on the pathway of gratitude.

Waging War against Control

It's not all flowers and unicorns though. The "daily bread" variety of prayers is also a battle cry, a declaration of war against one of the soul's fiercest enemies—control. Regardless of Enneagram number, Myers-Briggs type, stage of life, or upbringing, everyone wants control. Every last one of us lives with the insatiable desire to get control over our own lives, an inescapable attraction to that original lie, "You can be your own god."

Like every variety of fallenness, control is a good desire that is out of order. Control is a surface-level symptom of a soul-level desire for fruitfulness. We want to live consequential lives. We want to make a marked difference in the world, to matter in both a personal and profound way. But when we clinch our jaws and put that desire into action, we end up exhausted and overwhelmed. The millennial generation, of which I am a part, is the most socially conscious, globally minded, justice-oriented generation in recent memory. We are also the most mentally ill and chronically unhappy. We are a generation of people doing exactly what we want with our lives, channeling our energy freely into chosen pursuits for global good, and yet we are completely overwhelmed, utterly exhausted, and chronically anxious. Those are the symptoms of a good desire out of order.

Many have a subconscious, internal monologue that goes something like this: *I want to live a fruitful, meaningful life, but I'm just not sure I can trust God. I can trust him as my answer to the big theological questions, but I'm not sure if I can trust him with my dreams, my hopes, my plans. I can trust him ultimately, but I doubt I can trust him immediately. So, I'm white-knuckling my life with everything I've got— micromanaging my surroundings, my perception, my next step.*

When we trust God with our worldview but not our current experience in the world, we are falling victim to the lure of control.

How many of us are exhausted, overwhelmed, and chronically anxious because we're trying to satisfy good desires by the wrong means?

Luke's record of the Lord's Prayer is shorter, pithier than Matthew's. In Luke's recollection, which includes only five petitions, "daily bread" is the central, third request, the hinge on which the whole prayer turns. "Daily bread" is the heartbeat at the prayer's center.[8]

Jesus teaches us to include the phrase "give us" in our prayers. Daily, as we ask, he weans us off our addiction to independence, our insistence on living under the illusion that what we most deeply desire we can feed ourselves all on our own. Our requests are not the spoiled whining of a child or the shaking change cup of a beggar. Daily bread prayers are a daily reminder that we are not in charge, not in control.

Prayer replaces control with trust. A God-given desire is only fulfilled by God-given means.

I Want to Hear You Say It

There's a fascinating sequence in John 5 when Jesus approaches the Bethesda pool in Jerusalem. Ancient superstition was that this pool had healing powers; many believed that the first person to touch the waters with each bubbling swell received miraculous healing for their ailments.

When Jesus comes to that pool, he encounters a man who had been disabled for thirty-eight years. Jesus poses an interesting question: "Do you want to get well?"[9]

The question is equal parts tender and (forgive my irreverence) completely unnecessary. Isn't it obvious? He's a disabled man lying next to a healing pool. If you're Jesus, a rabbi with a reputation for miraculous healing, an invalid lying beside a healing pool is more or less a gimme.

It's like an EMT arriving on the scene of a car accident, running to the injured and bleeding, and asking the accident victim, "Do you want to get well?" "Are you kidding me? Why do I need to spell out the obvious?"

The unnecessary nature of the question is, of course, compounded by the fact that Jesus is the image of the invisible God. God—the One who knows what we need before we ask him (which is a phrase taken right from the lips of Jesus himself).[10] So when Jesus says to the invalid, "Do you want to get well?" it's like he's saying, "I want to hear you say it."

The same scene replays itself when Jesus turns water to wine at the wedding at Cana, when he raises the deceased daughter of the synagogue leader Jairus, and when he opens the eyes of the blind man Bartimaeus.[11] Jesus repeatedly poses questions that invite others to ask him for what they really want. "I want to hear you say it." Before acting, Jesus searches for consent.

From cover to cover, the Scriptures make this comprehensive point when it comes to prayer: God wants us to ask. He wants to hear you and me say it. As Charles Spurgeon points out, this rule even applies to Jesus himself: "Remember, *asking is the rule of the kingdom* . . . Remember this text, JEHOVAH says to His own Son, 'Ask me, and I will make the nations your inheritance . . .' [Psalm 2:8, quoted by Spurgeon in the KJV in his sermon]. If the royal and divine Son of God cannot be exempted from the rule of asking that He may have, you and I cannot expect the rule to be relaxed in our favor." He concludes, "If you may have everything by asking, and nothing without asking, I beg you to see how absolutely vital prayer is, and I beseech you to abound in it."[12]

Why is God so bent on asking? If he knows what we need before we ask him, why does he want us to ask him? I believe there are two primary reasons for God's insistence on hearing us say what he already knows we need: relationship and empowerment.

Relationship

The biblical story begins in relationship. Perfect relationship existed when there was nothing else—a completely sufficient triune God. Creation is born out of the abundant overflow of that loving relationship. The closest parallel we see to God's desire to create is a happily married couple so overjoyed in their union that they decide to have a baby. "Wouldn't it be amazing if a little bit of you and a little bit of me made a completely free, independent being, so that the love we share could be expressed and channeled toward another?" I imagine that was the motivation in the heart of God when he created man and woman in his image.

The biblical story ends in relationship. Currently, the work of the church includes mission, evangelism, perseverance, and justice, but a day will come when all those things will be done away with. Heaven, at its simplest, is eternity with God with no work left to do. The mission is accomplished, the evangelism done, justice the forever reality, and perseverance no longer needed. God's end game is just to be with you, to enjoy you forever, and to be enjoyed by you forever.

Communication is essential to relationship—particularly because asking insists on vulnerability. When you ask anyone for anything, you risk rejection or at least disappointment. Until we ask God for something, he can't disappoint or surprise us. We cannot build trust with God without asking. We can't relate to God if we never ask. Without asking, God is something less than a free, relational Being. He is a machine delivering on our desires, maybe even before we become conscious of what we want. Asking is the means by which we build the relationship with God he designed us to enjoy.

Jesus told a story about prayer that was surprising in its ordinariness and irreverence:

> Then Jesus said to them, "Suppose you have a friend, and you go to him at midnight and say, 'Friend, lend me three loaves of bread; a friend of mine on a journey has come to me, and I have no food to offer him.' And suppose the one inside answers, 'Don't bother me. The door is already locked, and my children and I are in bed. I can't get up and give you anything.' I tell you, even though he will not get up and give you the bread because of friendship, yet because of your shameless audacity he will surely get up and give you as much as you need." (Luke 11:5–8)

This story seems too common for the mystical action of prayer, but this is the story, straight from the divine imagination of Jesus, that illustrates petition.

This story is relational, as comfortably relational as ringing the neighbor's doorbell for a pinch off her sourdough starter or a few extra buns for a summer barbecue already underway. Talking to God is not an awkward meeting with an old, white-bearded monk where you try to think of something profound to say. Prayer is as casual as small talk. Asking is the experience of prayer at its most relational.

Empowerment

Relationship is God's end game, but empowerment is his plan for getting there. Jesus did not merely come to redeem the world but to invite the likes of us, fallen men and women, to participate in that redemption. There is perhaps no greater means of empowerment than petition.

Richard Foster writes, "We are not locked into a preset, determinist future. Ours is an open, not a closed, universe. We are 'co-laborers with God' . . . working with God to determine the outcome of events."[13] That's bound to make more than just a few readers squirm, but look no further than the Bible to discover the scandalous biblical claim of empowerment through prayer.

In Exodus 32, we get a glimpse into Moses's prayer life. To set the stage, God is very unhappy with the Israelites, and his anger is well-founded. After freeing them from slavery, parting the Red Sea, feeding them with bread from the sky, and quenching their thirst with water from a rock, they've begun to worship another god. God voices his anger, and in response, Moses prays, essentially calling God back to his own character:

> Turn from your fierce anger; relent and do not bring disaster on
> your people. Remember your servants Abraham, Isaac and Israel,
> to whom you swore by your own self: "I will make your descen-
> dants as numerous as the stars in the sky and I will give your
> descendants all this land I promised them, and it will be their
> inheritance forever." (Exodus 32:12–13)

Moses is holding God to his word. He's reminding God who God is: "by your own self." He's not just pleading with God to give him what he wants. It's more like he's reminding God what God really wants.

And check out God's response: "Then the LORD relented and did not bring on his people the disaster he had threatened."[14] Wait, what? Moses confronted God . . . and won? Yeah. Something like that.

The word *relented* is the translation of the Hebrew word *naham*, which can also be translated as "changed his mind" or even "repented." God *naham*ed. God changed his mind. God repented. Really? That's really what it says.[15]

This doesn't mean God was caught in sin and went to confession. *Naham* doesn't mean God was in the wrong. It means God was moved emotionally. Moses's prayer moved the Creator of the universe on an emotional level. That's what the Bible teaches.

Aristotle famously called God the "unmoved mover." The God Moses prayed to is more like the "moved mover." He's moving heaven and earth, but he's also movable. He hears us. He actually listens and actually cares. He responds. This idea of God may seem pretty radical, but that's only because many of us have a concept of God formed more by Aristotle than by Moses.

Don't get me wrong, there's a ton of mystery here. There are so many unanswered questions. Sure, that's how it happened with Moses, but what about Malachi? He heard God say, "I the Lord do not change."[16] But then there's Hosea, to whom God said, "My heart is changed within me; all my compassion is aroused."[17] How can both of these revelations of God be equally true? Because God is a relational being to know, not a formula to master.

When it comes to any relational being, we're gonna have to get comfortable with mystery. We will never know anyone so thoroughly that there's no mystery left. I will know and love my wife for the rest of my life, and I'll never reach the end of her. I'll never eliminate the mystery in my most intimate relationship.

Of course, it would be dangerous to form an entire theology out of this one Moses prayer, but there is a definite biblical pattern supported by this passage: God responds to his own character. That's his nature. John Mark Comer concludes, "God is more of a friend than a formula."[18]

The tendency in our modern churches is to strip the Bible of mystery and reduce it to abstractable principles. The tendency is to read something like Exodus 32 and think, *Wow, Moses and God really had something special there*, and then continue to lob half-hearted prayers up to Aristotle's god, as if Moses was some sort of superstar with different access to God than we have. In fact, Jesus said the opposite: "Whoever is least in my kingdom is greater than those who came before me."[19] To put the sentiment bluntly, "You are greater in God's eyes than Moses because you carry Jesus' authority when you pray."

The Bible is not a book to tell us how other people used to relate to God; it's a historical record of God's interaction with his people that should set the foundation and expectation for God's interaction with us. The prayers of Moses tell us definitively that God listens and God cares. God cares so much, in fact, that he's moved emotionally by our prayers.

Dallas Willard writes, "God's 'response' to our prayers is not a charade. He does not pretend he is answering our prayer when he is only doing what he was going to do anyway. Our requests really do make a difference in what God does or does not do."[20]

To those who think this is all just an Old Testament exception, and that after Moses, God got a stronger backbone and learned to stand his ground, take it up with the New Testament author James, who wrote pastorally to the common believer, "You do not have because you do not ask God."[21]

It is an inescapable New Testament reality that God freely shares his power with his sons and daughters. Of course, many times God uses prolonged waiting and even withholds power to form something essential in the inner life of the praying person. Equally, though, God shakes the temple floor beneath the feet of the gathered church, causes the paralyzed to stand, heals the sick, frees the addict, delivers the demonized, and throws open the cell doors of the imprisoned.

Good Gifts

Concluding his teaching on petition, Jesus says, "Which of you, if your son asks for bread, will give him a stone? Or if he asks for a fish, will give him a snake? If you, then, though you are evil, know how to give good gifts to your children, how much more will your Father in heaven give good gifts to those who ask him!"[22]

As an illustration of God's heart toward us in our asking, Jesus offers the image of a father who likes to give his kids what they need and want. In our world of such obvious brokenness and need, God enjoys not only redeeming wrongs but also giving us good gifts.

I distinctly remember coming home from a very long day last year. In a single day, I participated in a meeting of ministers mobilized to combat the still-prevalent systemic racism in the United States. I spoke with the largest food insecurity donor in New York City about the potential of making our local food pantry a full operation due to a growing hunger crisis in Brooklyn. I counseled a couple through discovered infidelity in their marriage that was producing broken trust and deep pain. With all the brokenness and need of our fallen world so apparent to me, when the elevator doors opened on the fourth floor and I jiggled my apartment keys from my pocket, I heard Simon's little voice from inside: "Dad's home!" He ran and hugged me when I walked in. Hank came out of his room and immediately asked, "Dad, can we have ice cream tonight?" I replied without even thinking, "Yeah buddy, let's have ice cream tonight."

The world is messed up. I'm doing my best to help more than I hurt. And still, in the face of all that brokenness and need, I like to give my kids ice cream. I love to say yes to what they want.

God is our Father. He's got a lot going on—a whole lot more than our minds can grasp at any given moment. And he still loves to give us what we want, even if it's parking spaces.

Ask. That's all he wants from us.

PRACTICE

Give Us Today Our Daily Bread

It is so freeing that in the middle of a prayer about heaven coming to earth and struggling against evil, Jesus throws in something as common as today's lunch. So let's honor him by bringing our everyday, ordinary requests, knowing he treasures those too.

Spend a few minutes praying for specific needs and wants in your life. I challenge you, especially, to ask for that which you think is too small to bring to God—the work meeting you're really hoping goes well, the need you barely believe God will meet, the email reply you keep checking your inbox for, the house you just put an offer on, or the rent check for which you don't have enough in your bank account to write.

Ask vulnerably, with enough specificity that God has the chance to disappoint you or surprise you. Ask boldly, with enough empowerment that you wonder if you're allowed to be this forward with God.

Chapter 7

THE MIDDLE VOICE
Prayer as Participation

*The assumption of spirituality is that always God
is doing something before I know it. So the task is
not to get God to do something I think needs to be
done, but to become aware of what God is doing
so that I can respond to it and participate and
take delight in it.*

Eugene Peterson, *The Contemplative Pastor*

Once we were inside, it was like being in the packed crowd of a pop concert, only these people were cramming through the doors to pray."

Alina was recounting her recent trip to Mumbai, where she waited in line for nearly an hour just to get into Siddhivinayak Temple, dedicated to Ganesha, a revered deity in the Hindu tradition. It was midday on a weekday, and the temple was busier than a suburban mall on Black Friday back in the United States. She and her husband had recently returned from a trip to India, and this was the experience she couldn't shake. The four of us sat around my kitchen table, our Chinese take-out containers steaming in front of us but no one taking a bite.

"I was rubbing shoulders with a frail elderly woman. She had to be in her eighties, and she had baked outside in the hot sun just to get in there," Alina went on, processing the experience aloud with us. "Now, she was crying out loudly as tears streamed down her cheeks, wailing in a language I didn't understand. And she wasn't alone. It was everyone. Every last one of them praying with more desperation and desire to a god I don't even believe exists than I've ever prayed to Jesus."

Our faith will be rocked when we see people praying with greater devotion to a false god than we pray to the one true God. Alina was reeling from that very experience. She had encountered prayer in its rawest, most active form.

Interestingly, likely just across the street or maybe a block away, one might find a Hindu temple filled with equally devoted people praying in nearly the opposite form. Hindus to some degree, and Buddhists particularly, pray by means of quiet, reverent meditation. The aim is self-emptying—letting go and surrendering to a divine other, an enlightened peace and serenity beyond themselves. This is prayer in its most passive, cerebral form.

Desperate wailing and quiet stillness, active and passive. Both are common expressions of prayer.

Most people know the active kind of prayer—trying to will God to adopt our own will. Usually with good motives, we try to usher in the action of God. We give our best, most compelling case, betraying the assumption that we need to talk God into something. And most of us also know the passive sort of prayer—trying to let God be and let ourselves simply be. We aren't asking for anything. In fact, we may be trying to empty ourselves of the desire to ask, attempting to reach a state of peace with what is.

The Bible itself records examples of active prayer. The Pharisees prayed in the context of personal morality, believing that if the whole Jewish nation could be obedient to the Torah's 613 commands for just a single day, the kingdom of God would come. The underlying presumption is there's a code we can crack. There's some combination of really meaning it, plus proving you really mean it, that gets God's ear.

Those who tire of that charade often turn to passive prayer. Praying in an attempt to empty oneself, becoming hollow and in harmony with the universe. Contemplation, though, understood biblically, is not about emptying but about being filled—blessed by the Father, clothed in Christ, filled with the Spirit.

Neither active nor passive prayer is how Jesus prayed.

The Middle Voice

Jesus prays in what Eugene Peterson calls "the middle voice."[1] In the active voice, I (the subject) am the actor. I initiate the action. "I give advice." In the passive voice, I (the subject) am being acted upon. I receive the action. "I am given advice." In ancient Greek, the language of the original New Testament, there's a third way of speaking—the middle voice. "I take advice." The middle voice means, "I am an active participant, but the action did not begin with me. I am *joining* the action of another."

Ancient Greek has, like Latin, been relegated to libraries and grad degrees, a language of academic study, but not common conversation between friends. That presents a pretty significant problem when it comes to learning prayer the way Jesus taught us because in English, we speak in either the active voice or the passive voice, but prayer takes place in the middle voice. Eugene Peterson, whose work is instrumental in defining these terms, writes:

Prayer and spirituality feature participation, the complex participation of God and the human, his will and our wills. We do not abandon ourselves to the stream of grace and drown in the ocean of love, losing identity. We do not pull strings that activate God's operations in our lives, subjecting God to our assertive identity. We neither manipulate God (active voice) nor are manipulated by God (passive voice). We are involved in the action and participate in its results but do not control or define it (middle voice). Prayer takes place in the middle voice.[2]

The middle voice means I am an active participant but the action began with another. We participate in the action, and we reap the benefits of the action. We are not entirely active. God's action doesn't depend on our initiative. Neither are we entirely passive. God has freely chosen to act almost exclusively in partnership with people. When we pray, we both participate in God's action and benefit from God's action. We *join* God. All of our interaction with God in prayer happens here—in the middle voice, the voice of participation.

Jesus not only taught us this way of prayer; he lived it. Take, for instance, Jesus' prayer in John 17: "My prayer is not for them alone. I pray also for those who will believe in me through their message, that all of them may be one, Father, just as you are in me and I am in you. May they also be in us so that the world may believe that you have sent me."[3] So an action that began with God ("just as you are in me and I am in you"), Jesus wants us to join and participate in ("may they also be in us")—the result of which is the world will see and believe. That's prayer in the middle voice.

Jesus keeps praying like this: "I have given them the glory that you gave me, that they may be one as we are one—I in them and you in me—so that they may be brought to complete unity. Then the world will know that you sent me and have loved them even as you have loved me."[4] Again, an action that began with God ("the glory that you gave me"), Jesus wants us to join and participate in ("that they may be brought to complete unity"), the result of which is, "The world will know that you sent me and have loved them." That's prayer in the middle voice, and that's what the praying voice of Jesus sounds like.

In Eden, the middle voice was the only form of communication. Adam and Eve were participants in God's action: naming the animals, harvesting the garden, generously ruling and reigning over every other species. None of what they were entrusted to steward began with them. Everything that is exists because God spoke the first word. But neither does God ask Adam and Eve to sit back and watch him rule. He invites their participation, even designing creation in such a way that it demands participation.

When Eve's teeth cut that crisp apple (or, more likely, that fig) from that one forbidden tree, it introduced the active voice into God's world. And when Adam, equally guilty, sheepishly passed the buck ("The woman you put here with me—she gave me some fruit from the tree, and I ate it"[5]), he introduced the passive voice into God's world.

The middle voice is the language of Edenic relationship. In prayer, Jesus invites us back into the relationship we knew in Eden at first and then lost in that first tragic act of deception. The assumption of biblical prayer is that God's action always precedes my request. The aim is not to get God in on what I think he should be doing. Rather, the aim of prayer is to get us in on what God is doing, become aware of it, join it, and enjoy the fruit of participation. Prayer is the recovery of our role in God's created order, the recovery of our true identity and the relationship that defines that identity to us.

Praying with Mary

Mary is a young girl, almost certainly a teenager, smitten with a boy and living into an imagined fairy-tale future. Idealistic, innocent Mary has just been paid a visit by an angel to inform her that she, a virgin, is carrying a child. The Spirit of God was the agent of conception, and Yahweh himself is the father.

On the one hand, this news is thrilling for Mary. God is finally making good on all those lofty promises the prophets chirped about centuries ago. *Not only is God keeping his promises,* Mary must have thought, *but he's keeping them in my days. I won't read the stories of the Messiah in a scroll; I'll watch them with my own two eyes. And if that weren't enough on its own, God has selected me for the cast in his redemption drama.* It's good news.

On the other hand, though, this news is devastating. Mary is engaged. Can you imagine trying to explain to Joseph that, yes, I'm pregnant with someone else's child, but not to worry, this someone else is the Alpha and Omega? Mary must assume that this news brings with it the cost of divorce and the broken heart of the man she loves. Then there's the legal issue. The Levitical laws list execution as the penalty for adultery. She lives in a small town. There's no keeping the news quiet. Unless she winds up with a particularly understanding fiancé and an unusually lenient judge, she's a single mother on death row by the end of the week. Her family will distance themselves from her. They'll have to, unless they want to be thrown out of the temple right along with her. Best-case scenario, she lives a quiet, lonely life with the permanent stain of social stigma and religious judgment. It's good news, but this good news sure is costly.

So Mary, with all of these thoughts ping-ponging in her mind as she listens to the angel's explanation, responds simply, "I am the Lord's servant. May your word to me be fulfilled."[6] It's a stunning prayer of surrender and participation. It's prayer in the middle voice among the mess of ordinary life.

Praying in the middle voice is a participation in the action of God. It is an acknowledgment of our place in his created order, recipients of his action and responders to it. God's activity is like the current of the Mississippi River. We can agree with it, enter into it, and swim freely along with the water's pull. We can also deny his activity, swim against the current, and fight it with the flailing of our arms and kicking of our feet. Either way, we're going with the river. No one wins a fight against that kind of current. You can agree with it and cruise along assisted, or you can fight it and be pushed along, exhausted. The one thing you can't do is pretend the rushing river current is a still-water pond.

When Mary prayed with staggering faith, "I am the Lord's servant. May your word to me be fulfilled," she was transforming her everyday tasks—doctor visits, proper nutrition, and three trimesters of discomfort—into a participation in God's redemption. She was cooperating with God's activity in the world and within her. The result was divine blessing: "From now on all generations will call me blessed."[7]

I want that too. I want what I see in Mary. I want to cooperate with God's redemptive work in this broken world. I want to swim with the current, speeding along effortlessly, paddling my arms and kicking my legs but propelled on by a stronger current too. I want to cooperate with God's work in me, inviting his formation of my desires, thoughts, emotions, and actions, all of them hopelessly disordered by the fallen lineage of which I'm a part. I want the Spirit of God to rework me from within, like an expert mechanic to a classic car, getting me running according to design.

There's a phrase in Psalm 112 I hardly go a week without pondering: "Surely the righteous will never be shaken; they will be remembered forever. They will have no fear of bad news; their hearts are steadfast, trusting in the LORD."[8] No fear of bad news? Can you even imagine living with that sort of resilience? My psyche is fragile. There's nothing I fear like bad news. Daily, I fall for the illusion that peace is having all the scattered parts of my life in just the right order, under the illusion of my own control. The very second "my plan" is thwarted by life's unpredictability, fear plunges into my gut like an Olympic diver.

With that angelic appearance, the life Mary had been piecing together, the future plan she had been anticipating, seemed to be demolished, shattered into countless tiny shards. And what's her response? "I am the Lord's servant. May your word to me be fulfilled." That's a resilience I don't have, but I want it.

Prayer is the means by which we open our inner world to the Spirit's work within us and say, "Yes, have your way." By praying in the middle voice, we consent to the deep work of the Spirit within, deeper even than language, forming us into resilient people in a fragile world, with no fear of bad news.

Praying with Jesus

On the opposite end of Luke's gospel, when the story that began with Mary's middle voice prayer is drawing to a close, Jesus prayed nearly identical words: "Father, if you are willing, take this cup from me; yet not my will, but yours be done."[9] The life of God, which was received in prayer by Mary, is lived in prayer by Jesus. On the most anguish-ridden, defining night of his life, Jesus prays the words of his mother. He must have heard her pray it as a child, Creator steeped in the praying voice of his own creation. And I can't help but wonder if when faced with the mess of redemption in a fallen world, Jesus didn't think of his mom, finding resilience at the end of his life in the very place she had found it at the beginning.

Do you know this life of consenting participation? As time passes and your own lack of control becomes more apparent, are you growing in resilience, or in anxiety? Are your prayers mostly the entitled demands of the active voice, insisting on deliverance from circumstances that don't align with your plan? Or might your prayers be the apathetic mumblings of the passive voice, acting out a part in a spiritual drama in which you don't actually believe you have a consequential, participatory role?

Discover prayer in the middle voice. God is sovereign, but his is a participatory sovereignty. "The better a man learns to pray," writes Hans Urs von Balthasar, "the more deeply he finds that all his stammering is only an answer to God's speaking to him."[10]

The Collateral Damage of Intimacy

Praying as Jesus taught us, in the middle voice, is both a restored identity as God's chosen partners (within the praying person) and participation in God's gracious work of re-creation (in the world around the praying person). It should be noted, then, that prayer is a risky business. In my experience, God has a habit of employing us in response to our own prayers.

And you don't have to take my word for it. Mother Teresa, surely one of the most broadly respected Christ followers of the last century, rejected any view of her life as an activist. In her Nobel Prize acceptance speech, she claimed that anyone who viewed her life as being about social work or even compassion had it backward. In reality, she claimed that she, along with her fellow servants, were nothing more than "contemplatives in the heart of the world."[11]

She was saying that everything she was being awarded for—caring for the poor, rehabilitating the addicts, creating a community of heavenly love in a poor slum—all of it just accidentally happened in response to prayer.

In other words, her life was about being with God and responding accordingly. Social justice was simply the natural response to being with Jesus. Mother Teresa wasn't an activist; she was a person of prayer—prayer in the middle voice. All of her active ministry was nothing more than recognizing and joining an action that began with God. Prayer, properly understood and practiced, is the seed from which fruitfulness grows.

Intimacy leads to fruitfulness, not the other way around. Those who prioritize a loving relationship with God, meeting with him in prayer through stolen moments throughout the day, long stretches of disciplined contemplation, and fiery pleas of intercession, are those with whom he shares his divine power.

Jesus himself said, "This is to my Father's glory, that you bear much fruit."[12] But fruit comes from intimacy. Fruitfulness comes because we love Jesus and want to be with him. When that's our heart, the expression of that relationship begins to look like justice in the world, compassion for others, and peace in our inner being. It is symptomatic of spiritual dysfunction to spend time with Jesus and not be employed in the answer to our own prayers.

Biblically speaking, inner prayer and outward compassion are inseparable. The Hebrew term for personal righteousness is *tsedaqah*, and the Hebrew term for outward justice is identical—*tsedaqah*. That's crucial because it implies that the historic biblical understanding of devotion to God was this: to be righteous is to care for the poor, and to care for the poor is to be righteous, which is why prophets like Isaiah and Amos got so worked up about people who were inwardly devout but outwardly disengaged. In the ancient Hebrew understanding of righteousness, a community of pious, private spiritual practice without equal devotion to costly public compassion was not only dysfunctional but oxymoronic.

Jesus famously confronted the priests of his day in Luke 11: "You Pharisees clean the outside of the cup and dish, but inside you are full of greed and wickedness."[13] It was a stinging accusation, maybe one he'd levy just as strongly at us. But pay attention to the antidote he prescribed for a personal righteousness devoid of mercy in the verses that follow: "But now as for what is inside you—be generous to the poor, and everything will be clean for you."[14] A life of faith without mercy is a kingdom the King doesn't recognize. It's impossible to know God through private prayer without equally participating with God in public mercy.

Prayer and mission fit together, hand in glove. To pray is to be invited to uncomfortable mission. To pray is to be led by the hand to broken places, broken people, and broken parts within yourself. Jesus feels at home in the company of the misfits, marginalized, oppressed, and outcast, so if you spend time in conversation with Jesus, you better believe he'll invite you to come with him where he's going. N. T. Wright writes, "The Christian vocation is to be in prayer, in the Spirit, at the place the world is in pain."[15] Proximity to pain lends credibility and power to our prayers.

We must keep in mind, though, that when we make fruitfulness the goal, leapfrogging intimacy, we make a well-intentioned but tragic mistake. When we try to carry out the mission of Jesus without grounding every action in intimacy with Jesus, we will often come out of the gate strong. A lot of social good has been done in our world through gritted teeth and the caring heart of a serious activist. However, more often than not, this motivation does not end in kingdom fruit. Even though it often starts that way, it tends to end in exhaustion and resentment.

One of the greatest tragedies I've observed in the church is that those who in the name of Jesus become the most dedicated to social activism often start with pure hearts, but somewhere along the way, many end up cold and judgmental toward the church. The work of mercy is often taken up by those most unmerciful to their brothers and sisters. The problem is not the work of compassion, mercy, and justice; rather, the problem is the pursuit of fruitfulness apart from an equal pursuit of intimacy. Prayer is the furnace that fuels mission.

When we pray with Jesus, we—almost accidentally—start doing the sorts of things Jesus did. It's like we can't help it. Intimacy in prayer is the way to lasting fruitfulness.

Our lives are about intimacy. Fruitfulness is the collateral gain of that intimacy.

PRACTICE

Praying with Mary

"I am the Lord's servant. May your word to me be fulfilled."[16]

This is prayer in the middle voice. Let Mary's prayer serve as a template for your own, her words beginning a train of thought with God that you add to thematically and spontaneously.

Praying Mary's words is like riding a bike with training wheels. We use these phrases as guards for a while as we get used to the feel of balancing on two wheels, which feels like a tightrope at first. But training wheels are always designed to come off. As we pray Mary's prayer, these movements become our own. All of our prayers become the participatory sort of prayer Jesus taught us as we go. But we must start slowly and deliberately.

"I Am the Lord's Servant"

The first statement is one of identity. It is a reminder of my place in God's created order. The persistent mantra of the Western world, even within the church, is a barrage of self-inflation: "You are more important than you ever dreamed. God has a tailor-made destiny for you and wants to use your life for great things!" Of course, there's a lot of truth in that. However, in the face of that nonstop reminder, I am deeply comforted in remembering that I popped into a story where I'm not playing the lead. I'm an extra in the background of a single scene in a narrative that is grander, more complex, and more redemptive than I could fathom. This is a story about God. He is the lead, at the center of every scene. I am the Lord's *servant*. And that, as it turns out, is more than enough for me.

Yet I am *the Lord's* servant. I belong to the King of kings and serve in the kingdom that outlasts all the others. There is no voice, no force, no condemnation that can make me any less than his.

Begin your prayer by reminding yourself of this humble but profoundly dignifying identity. Let go of all self-inflation and flattery. Equally, let go of all dejection, self-doubt, and insecurity. You are a servant, and you belong to the Lord himself.

"May Your Word to Me Be Fulfilled"

The second statement is one of vocation and participation. It is a consent to the Spirit's work both in and through me. To pray these words is to search the circumstances I am living in today (typically circumstances I'd like to make some adjustments to) for God's invitation. It is to say yes to God's formation within me, making me a gift of love to the world, an answer to my own most audacious prayers. It is also a yes to God's work through me, calling me to a particular role in his ongoing redemption right now, today. Consent to the work of God is acceptance and participation—acceptance that God is here and now in this moment, these circumstances, these relationships; participation in God's invitation when I recognize him here in the mess.

Move now to prayers of consent. Wherever you recognize God at work in your inner life, thank him for it, and ask that he will complete the work he has begun, remaking you into his image. Wherever you recognize his Spirit inviting you to act, say yes. Commit to go, to give, to forgive, to include, to slow down, to rest, to see, to hope, to believe, to serve, to speak, to listen, to wait, to love.

Chapter 8

LABORING IN PRAYER

Praying for the Lost

> *And Elijah said to Ahab, "Go, eat and drink, for*
> *there is the sound of a heavy rain." So Ahab went*
> *off to eat and drink, but Elijah climbed to the top*
> *of Carmel, bent down to the ground and put his*
> *face between his knees.*
>
> 1 Kings 18:41–42

D. L. Moody, a late nineteenth–century traveling preacher, was one of the most influential evangelists in the modern church era. He was one of nine children born to a single mother who struggled to keep food on the table. A shoe salesman in Boston with only a fifth-grade education, Moody came to faith at seventeen and began preaching to overlooked and marginalized teens shortly afterward. He went on to travel the world, drawing crowds as large as thirty thousand to hear his sermons. Many consider him to have been the greatest evangelist of the nineteenth century.

While the fruitfulness of his ministry speaks for itself, his methodology was neither innovative nor impressive. We've grown accustomed these days to witnessing swells of salvation—the lost being found, the outsider coming in, new children born into the family of Jesus—through innovation, a new strategy or technique. A new tool comes along like the *Jesus* film, the Alpha Course, a weekend revival effort, or a church-sponsored short-term mission trip, and that tool spearheads a surge in evangelism. There's usually a novel method somewhere near the center of the explanation of why evangelism is "working" (for lack of a better term).

Moody's life and ministry is a compelling exception to the rule. His entire evangelistic strategy was prayer. That's it. In an oft-told legend, many before me have recounted that Moody famously carried a list of a hundred names in his pocket every day of his adult life—one hundred friends who had no relationship with Jesus. Moody's labor of love was secret, hidden prayer on their behalf. He pleaded with God to reveal himself to each of them in a way they could perceive and receive as eternal love. He prayed by name for their salvation.

When he died, ninety-six of the names on that list had become answered prayers. A 96 percent success rate in prayer is not bad. I'd take those odds any day of the week. But it gets better. At Moody's funeral, the four remaining names were each in attendance. Those four friends were, independently, so moved by the memorial service that they all came to faith—at his funeral![1]

So just for the record, how did a shoe salesman with a fifth-grade education become one of the most influential evangelists in recorded history? Prayer.

When I first heard that story, a surge of inspiration and resolve swept over me. I started to keep a list of friends, set alerts on my phone that would remind me to pray for them, and dedicated my life to the secret labor of loving prayer that I witnessed in Moody.

A few weeks later, I told this story in a sermon I was preaching at the church I led at the time. I challenged the community, and we agreed together, "Let's do this. Let's pray—not for the idea of people or even for people groups—but for individual people, names and faces we know personally and interact with regularly. Let's live like D. L. Moody lived, and see what God does!"

Nine months after that challenge, I told Moody's story again the same way to the same church. Then I asked a simple question, "How many of you are still doing it? Praying daily for at least one name, living like D. L. Moody?" One hand. In a sea of committed, lovely, well-meaning, and sincere followers of Jesus—just one. And it wasn't my hand either. I made it for a month or two, and then a daily practice became every once in a while, and that, of course, was a slippery slope to prayer alerts on my phone screen that became habitually ignored and swiped away.

That doesn't make me or the community I pastor failures; it makes us normal. Everyone I know has a low success rate in praying for the lost (meaning those who haven't been found in the new family of Jesus)—everyone. Everyone I know has low stamina in praying for the lost. And then, every once in a while, you'll hear an inspiring sermon about an old woman (why is it always an elderly woman?) who prayed and prayed for the same person for thirty years before finally seeing a breakthrough. We get inspired by those stories, but inspiration wears thin in the course of ordinary life, and even the most resolute willpower is a depleted resource.

And yet it is an undeniable biblical theme that prayer gives birth to new life. And I know how unfashionable it is to talk of our following Jesus as being "born again." Some guy with a fiery sign and a bullhorn in Times Square has made that a bad look for all of us. But biblically speaking, that's the richest, most consistent metaphor for salvation.

Prayer Gives Birth to New Life

The mysterious, long, and slow process of spiritual birth is seeded by prayer. This theme is found all over the Bible but is vividly pictured in the life of the prophet Elijah. Let's retrace his story in three scenes.

Scene 1: The Church on Fire

> Then the fire of the LORD fell and burned up the sacrifice, the wood, the stones and the soil, and also licked up the water in the trench.
>
> When all the people saw this, they fell prostrate and cried, "The LORD—he is God! The LORD—he is God!" (1 Kings 18:38–39)

Israel has forgotten God (they tend to do that). The Old Testament pattern is that of an Israel that looks to Yahweh out of desperation, who then responds. When desperation is replaced by safety and comfort, however, they tend to put their trust in something more tangible and predictable, something requiring less faith. In Elijah's time, trust is vested in a king named Ahab and his wife, Jezebel, who led Israel away from Yahweh and into idol worship of a false god called Baal.

In a moment of extraordinary courage, Elijah says, essentially, "Not on my watch!" He approaches the king and issues a challenge: "I'm one prophet of Yahweh. There are 450 prophets of Baal. Let's set up a sacrifice with two altars—one to Yahweh, another to Baal. Put a bull on the altar [this sort of animal sacrifice was standard form for all kinds of worship to all kinds of supposed gods in the ancient Near Eastern world]. But do not set fire to the sacrifice. Instead, pray. We'll see whose god answers by sending fire from heaven to light the sacrifice. The god who sends fire is the one, true God."[2]

Those were the intriguing terms that caught Ahab's attention. No matter which side you're on, people rarely put themselves out there like this. The king couldn't resist.

The sacrifices are set up, and the 450 prophets of Baal go first. They pray, and nothing happens. They grow more intense, shouting and chanting. Nothing happens. Eventually, they begin to cut themselves, mutilating their bodies to get their god's attention. Nothing happens. These 450 prophets exhaust themselves praying to Baal most of the day. Nothing happens.

Now it's Elijah's turn. Before praying, "he repaired the altar of the Lord, which had been torn down."[3] Elijah walks over to the old altar of Yahweh, the one that had been torn down in the name of Baal, and rebuilds on the very foundation where Israel used to worship. The symbolism is significant.

Then he says to the people who gathered, "Fill four large jars with water and pour it on the offering and on the wood."[4] On the surface, this seems impressive because wet wood is obviously more difficult to burn, but Elijah is not Houdini setting up a magic trick; he is a worshiper preparing to pray.

Israel is three years into a drought—not a drop of rain has fallen in more than a thousand days. That would be an issue today, limiting agriculture, encouraging wildfires, altering the ecosystem. But in an agrarian society without a sophisticated trade system between nations? This is devastating. The country is starving to death, and no political policy or change in power can do anything about it. Water. They need water. In the meantime, conventional wisdom dictates conserving as much water as possible. Limit bathing. Drink only what you have to. Save it for the crops. Water is the most limited resource and prized possession in a drought.

This means water is the costliest offering Elijah could bring. He places not only his reputation before God and this crowd but also his livelihood, his security, his future well-being. The most profound act of worship and faith occurs before a word of prayer when this prophet pours out a cistern of the most precious national commodity over the wood. The words of David echo over the scene: "I will not sacrifice to the LORD my God burnt offerings that cost me nothing."[5] Then Elijah says, "Now do it again. And for good measure, soak it one more time." He is offering God the most lavish sacrifice he can possibly bring. That's significant.

Finally, Elijah prays, "'Answer me, LORD, answer me, so these people will know that you, LORD, are God, and that you are turning their hearts back again.' Then the fire of the LORD fell and burned up the sacrifice, the wood, the stones and the soil, and also licked up the water in the trench. When all the people saw this, they fell prostrate and cried, 'The LORD—he is God! The LORD—he is God!'"[6]

Take in all that has just happened. Elijah has repaired the altar, restoring the place of worship. Elijah has poured out water, which was not only precious to him but an involuntary sacrifice for everyone gathered, making all who came as spectators become participants in worship. Next, God's presence has become obvious. Fire fell where a moment ago there had been nothing but wet wood and red meat. At that, the people return to God. People who helped tear down the altar of Yahweh are now facedown worshiping him by name.

Call to mind that family member, friend, or coworker you perceive to be farthest from God—the one you don't even bother to pray for or consider inviting into a relationship with the Lord, the one before whom you actively avoid the faith subject. Imagine that person sitting next to you on an otherwise sleepy Sunday morning in the old familiar sanctuary. Only today, as you're singing, she falls to the ground and begins screaming out, "The LORD—he is God! The LORD—he is God!" Can you imagine witnessing something like that? A visible manifestation of God's presence followed by people who had been hostile to God falling facedown in worship? If that were to happen at your local church, I'm sure you'd leave pleasantly surprised by your worship experience. It seems fair to say that the church had just caught fire.

But that's not the end; it's just the beginning. Because God doesn't dream of the church on fire, and this isn't the climactic moment of Elijah's story.

It'll make sense if you know the end, so let's skip ahead.

Scene 3: The City Reborn

> And Elijah said to Ahab, "Go, eat and drink, for there is the sound of a heavy rain." (1 Kings 18:41)

It's worth keeping in mind that Elijah is a prophet talking to a desperate political leader—the national leader of a starving people. Under his leadership, the economy has collapsed, people have suffered, and blame and criticism has surely come knocking at the palace door.

Ahab's desperation, though, would be just a fragment of the majority peasant class's. Ahab is likely still eating fresh baked bread and stew from the royal storehouses. The common people of the city have run out of rations. Like the horror stories of villages ravaged by Nazi Germany, the surviving class is left to make decisions about who to feed—the mother or the baby, grandpa or the children.

And in the midst of that situation, Elijah locks eyes with the king and says confidently, "Go and celebrate. Slaughter the fattened calf, fire up the grill, and uncork that bottle you've been saving because God is about to give reason for celebration. The God you just saw light up the drenched altar with holy fire—he's now gonna provide sustenance for the whole city."

So Ahab went off to eat and drink, but Elijah climbed to the top of Carmel, bent down to the ground and put his face between his knees.

"Go and look toward the sea," he told his servant. And he went up and looked.

"There is nothing there," he said.

Seven times Elijah said, "Go back."

The seventh time the servant reported, "A cloud as small as a man's hand is rising from the sea."

So Elijah said, "Go and tell Ahab, 'Hitch up your chariot and go down before the rain stops you.'"

Meanwhile, the sky grew black with clouds, the wind rose, a heavy rain started falling and Ahab rode off to Jezreel. (1 Kings 18:42–45)

Three years into a drought, a massive downpour deluges the city, a celebration breaks out in the streets, and new life springs up in a depressed place. This is the climactic moment in Elijah's story.

God doesn't dream of the church on fire; God dreams of the city reborn. God's dream isn't that the church will improve its programs, grow in number, add another worship service, and host an influential conference. All of that is fine. It's just not what God dreams about. God dreams about pouring his Spirit out on the whole city.

God is jealous.[7] He's jealous for relationship. He jealously longs for every last soul because he created each one individually and uniquely. He jealously longs for every ounce of his creation. As Abraham Kuyper so startlingly put it, "There is not a square inch in the whole domain of our human existence over which Christ, who is Sovereign over *all*, does not cry: 'Mine!'"[8]

God dreams of a city reborn. And Elijah's story tells us clearly that dream starts with a church on fire, but that's just the beginning of the journey, not the destination. The city reborn—that's the destination. Every journey worth taking must have an origin and an arrival, and we should not confuse the two. There is no successful adventure without a known destination. A church on fire is the vehicle that gets us moving toward God's true longing—a city reborn.

The journey between the starting place and destination is long and winding and not without significant detour. That's why the beginning and ending aren't enough. We must take scene 2, the middle of the journey, seriously and practically.

Scene 2: The Mountain of Prayer

> So Ahab went off to eat and drink, but Elijah climbed to the top of Carmel, bent down to the ground and put his face between his knees. (1 Kings 18:42)

Elijah sends the king off to prepare for rain, and then what does he do? He climbs a mountain and begins to pray. He hikes to the peak, takes in the view overlooking the desperate city that God loves, and prays like this: "Elijah . . . bent down to the ground and put his face between his knees."

That's an odd posture for prayer. Frequently in the Bible, we encounter people falling facedown, prostrate in prayer or kneeling in humility. Jesus often prayed on mountaintops with his eyes open as he hiked or watched the sun rise over the city. But Elijah "bent down to the ground and put his face between his knees."

Whenever there's a specific detail in the Bible, one that seems gratuitous or strange, lean in and pay close attention. There are no unimportant details in the Scripture. Taken simply as a work of literature, the Bible tends to gloss over details. It's written more in the style of someone furiously trying to keep up than like a novelist dreaming up a story and editing it several times over. In 1 Kings, we're told, "Then the fire of the LORD fell and burned up the sacrifice."[9] That's enough for us to get the picture. But if a novelist had written it? It would've sounded more like, "Then the flames danced across the splintered oak like someone just put on the 'Cha-Cha Slide' at an Anglo-Saxon wedding reception."

So why the detailed description of Elijah's abnormal prayer posture? Because it tells us something important. To pray for the city, Elijah metaphorically gets into the position of a woman in labor, beginning to push.

I know. It's graphic. Even the New Testament writer James, referring to this event, called it, "fervent" or "effectual" prayer.[10] More recently, this laborious method of prayer is commonly referred to as "travailing " or "contending" prayer. Whatever you call it, here's the point: there is a kind of prayer that gives birth to new life.

There Is a Kind of Prayer That Gives Birth to New Life

All the way back on page 1 of the story, we read, "Now the earth was formless and empty, darkness was over the surface of the deep, and the Spirit of God was hovering over the waters."[11] The Hebrew word translated here as "formless" is *tohu*, which can also be translated as "barren."[12] Creation happens when the Spirit gives life to a barren place. God's original creation is explained through the imagery of childbirth.

After the fall, when God wanted to redeem the world, he started again with a barren womb—that of Sarah—and her husband, Abraham. In the beginning, the Spirit hovered over barren chaos to bring forth creation. In redemption, the same

Spirit hovers over the barren womb of Sarah to begin the work of re-creation.

When God finally enters the story himself, he comes through childbirth. "The Holy Spirit will come on you, and the power of the Most High will overshadow you," said the angel to the virgin Mary.[13] The same Spirit hovers over another womb. The Holy Spirit works miracles at the opposite ends of the stage-of-life spectrum, each resulting in new life in a fallen world, re-creation in the midst of a broken and dysfunctional creation. The miracle of Isaac's birth to Sarah was medical. A barren womb was opened up by the Holy Spirit. The miracle of Jesus' birth to Mary was biological. A virgin womb was fertilized by the Holy Spirit. And the angel's message to Mary, providing a bit of necessary context for what's happening within her, sounds nearly identical to Genesis 1 and God's promise to Abraham and Sarah in Genesis 17.

On the final night of his life, Jesus describes his approaching death, his three days in a tomb, and his resurrection through the imagery of childbirth: "A woman giving birth to a child has pain because her time has come; but when her baby is born she forgets the anguish because of her joy that a child is born into the world."[14]

Jesus promises to fill all who will receive him with his very Spirit—the same Spirit that gave birth to new life at creation, new life in redemption through Sarah, new life in incarnation through Mary, and new life in resurrection through Jesus. Jesus promises his creating Spirit to all: "'Whoever believes in me, as Scripture has said, rivers of living water will flow from within them.' By this he meant the Spirit, whom those who believed in him were later to receive."[15] The English phrase "within them" comes from the single Greek word *koilia*, which has as one of its meanings the word *womb*.[16] Jesus calls you and me the "womb" that God's Spirit inhabits to create new life.

The undeniable biblical theme is this: there is a kind of prayer that gives birth to new life. And this is the sort of prayer God loves to answer—prayers for new life, prayers for salvation.

God doesn't only dream of a church on fire; God dreams of a city reborn. A mountain of prayer is the only way from one to the other.

But if you ascend this mountain of prayer, proceed with caution. Because here's the bit you likely already know by experience: prayer for the lost is slow and unglamorous.

Prayer for the Lost Is Slow

"Go and look toward the sea," he told his servant. And he went up and looked.

"There is nothing there," he said.

Seven times Elijah said, "Go back."

The seventh time the servant reported, "A cloud as small as a man's hand is rising from the sea." (1 Kings 18:43–44)

Elijah prayed for fire once; he prayed for rain seven times. The sort of prayer that gives birth to new life is slow. Perhaps you had a friend you sensed God was pursuing. And then you had a memorable conversation when they seemed open to belief. Excitedly, you started to pray more. Nothing happened.

Then seven weeks, seven months, maybe seven years, or even decades into fervent prayer for that one person, finally there was something! Some glimmer of hope that maybe God was at work, mysteriously drawing their heart to him and weaving the circumstances of their life to expose his unquenchable love for them as you prayed and prayed and kept on praying.

My oldest son, Hank, was born in a hospital-housed birthing center in lower Manhattan. If you're unfamiliar with the terminology, a birthing center is more or less a small hotel room inside a busy hospital. Instead of the medical jargon, frantic nurses, and busy labor and delivery doctors frequently associated with hospital births, birth centers are run by midwives, most often the baggy-hemp-wearing, chamomile-tea-sipping, gently whispering variety (to paint you a bit of a picture).

Eight hours into the labor, there was some discomfort. Kirsten's was absolutely agonizing, but I was beginning to get hungry—slight discomfort.

It was at this precise point in the labor that I decided to remove the footlong Italian sub I had strategically stowed away in the minifridge eight hours earlier. I took the first bite and heard what sounded like the voice of a Pixar animated dragon call loudly from the other side of the room: "What's that smell?" That's when I knew the "slight discomfort" of my hunger was here to stay.

Ten hours into labor, the midwife finally asked, "Kirsten, are you ready to have this baby?" She was encouraged. I was elated! The bread would be soggy by now, but the sandwich was still salvageable.

She started pushing. She kept pushing. Kept pushing. It would be eight more hours before we met Hank. And during those long hours, she experienced more pain than she ever had before. No other human feat compares to the courage of a mother-to-be in labor. Kirsten had moments where she thought it was time, but there was still a long way to go. She had points along the way where she wanted to give up but bravely continued. More than once, she said to anyone listening, "I'm never doing this again."

Then we met Hank. About a week after the eighteen-hour birth—no exaggeration on the timeline—she said, "Tyler, I want another baby." It was like all the worst moments from the labor had been washed away by the joy of new life. Whatever she went through—this guy, this little guy who so far had only caused her excruciating pain, greatly inconvenienced her sleep patterns, and promised to be completely dependent on us both for years to come—was so worth it.

Jesus said, "When her baby is born she forgets the anguish because of her joy that a child is born into the world." New life requires labor—laboring in prayer. But the joy of salvation always far outweighs the preceding pain, struggle, and persistence. Plenty of people have been inspired by D. L. Moody's list of one hundred people. Far fewer people continued to pray after the inspiration wore off. If you want that kind of legacy, you've got to live that kind of life. Birthing prayer is slow.

Prayer for the Lost Is Unglamorous

Calling fire down from heaven won Elijah public admiration. There must've been a stir in the crowd, his name on every tongue. Praying a downpour on the city, by contrast, was a secret labor—unseen and unglamorous. It's the secret labor of prayer, not the public spectacle of fire, we are told to imitate.

There's one moment when Jesus' disciples seem interested in re-creating Elijah's fire spectacle: "When the disciples James and John saw this, they asked, 'Lord, do you want us to call fire down from heaven to destroy them?' But Jesus turned and rebuked them. Then he and his disciples went to another village."[17] That's a firm and straightforward no.

It is the secret, unglamorous part of Elijah's life we are biblically instructed to imitate. James 5 reads, "The prayer of a righteous person is powerful and effective. Elijah was a human being, even as we are. He prayed earnestly that it would not rain, and it did not rain on the land for three and a half years. Again he prayed, and the heavens gave rain, and the earth produced its crops."[18] We have an appetite for spectacle; God has an appetite for new life. We can't resist public spectacle; God can't resist the secret labor of prayer.

Plenty of those in today's church would say, "I want to be there when the fire falls! I want to see revival! Bring on the signs and wonders!" Far fewer are ready to labor in secret prayer. It's not glamorous. But it is powerful and effective.

God wants the church on fire *because* God dreams of the city reborn. God is delighted by a growing passion for worship within a believing community. Elijah repaired the altar before calling for fire. God is glorified by instances of costly sacrifice—pouring cisterns of water over the altar during a drought. And in those instances when the church gathers to worship and pray and the fire falls, Jesus is there, dancing with a supernatural smile stretched across his face. God ignites the church because he's jealous for the city.

Elijah's story and James's call to participation in prayer are invitations for us to be found by God on the mountain of prayer, to join with the Holy Spirit in groaning for new life. It requires us to be persistent and single-minded and to develop an acquired taste for the unglamorous. To accept this invitation requires us to display a stubborn willingness to pray through the waiting, a supernatural labor of willful agony for the promise of new life.

The Pattern of Renewal

Every great move of God in church history, every revival and awakening, follows a common pattern: the church catches fire, leading to an increased priority of prayer, resulting in an outpouring of the Spirit on a city. In the words of J. Edwin Orr, "Whenever God is ready to do something new with His people, He always sets them to praying."[19]

Charles Spurgeon is arguably the most famous preacher in

history. Whenever he was asked his secret, he always pointed to a team of intercessors who prayed nonstop throughout his sermons. During every second that Spurgeon preached, his intercessors prayed. His church had a small room directly beneath the stage and pulpit where the intercessors gathered to pray through the duration of his teaching. Spurgeon called it his "boiler room."[20] Asked for rhetorical tips, Spurgeon essentially only ever gave one piece of advice: God has a soft spot for the unglamorous, secret work of prayer.

The influence of Spurgeon's prayer-saturated messages is remarkable. The story is told, for example, a British prisoner in a South American prison was paid a visit by a British friend who gifted him with two novels. Amazingly, a Spurgeon sermon was wedged between the leaves of one of the novels. After reading the sermon, right then and there, inside a foreign jail cell, he surrendered his life to Christ.[21]

Similarly, the biographer Lewis Drummond reported the story of a rural shepherd, who while walking in the bush in Ballarat, Australia, found a leaf of a newspaper that had been blown around by the wind. Picking it up, he noticed that one of the pages looked like an advertisement, but it happened to have nearly all of a Spurgeon sermon printed on it. The shepherd read every word of it, and alone in a field he surrendered his life to Jesus. Drummond wrote, "The man confessed that if he had realized the article was a sermon, he would never have read it. But seeing it in the newspaper in the form of an advertisement, he became interested, read it, and found Christ."[22]

So what was your secret, Dr. Spurgeon? How can we learn to wax eloquently like you did and get the results you got?

Oh, it's not what you think, he might say. *I've got this team of intercessors who pray unceasingly while I preach.* In other words, there's a kind of prayer that gives birth to new life.

Prayer is slow and unglamorous and it sometimes requires labor pains, but prayer is also a means to the joy of new life.

PRACTICE

Labor in Prayer

Ask God to allow you to see your daily routine from his divine perspective. Let your eyes run imaginatively over your day-to-day life—the colleagues you work with, the circle of friends you socialize with, the acquaintances you routinely breeze past. Invite the Holy Spirit to walk you through your average week and let you imaginatively see life through the eyes of a wholly loving, ever-pursuing God.

As you see your life from his perspective, whom do you notice? Is there someone God is pursuing whom you're overlooking? Someone you are counting out whom God is inviting you to notice?

Jot down a few names—at least one—that God brings to mind. Carry around in your pocket a piece of paper with those names, set a daily reminder on your phone, create a digital sticky note on your desktop or phone background, write them on your bathroom mirror. Whatever works for you.

Pray for that name or names. Pray specifically enough that you'll know if God answers your prayer, and regularly enough that endurance and labor are required.

Along the way, you may need to ask God for a renewed faith that he's actually listening or for a renewed compassion for the individuals you're praying for. Don't let this activity be diminished to an item on an agenda. Ask for faith, hope, and love to be your motivation as you go, and ask for new life to be the result of this laboring prayer.

Chapter 9

ASK, SEEK, KNOCK

Silence and Persistence

Ask and it will be given to you; seek and you will
find; knock and the door will be opened to you.
For everyone who asks receives; the one who
seeks finds; and to the one who knocks, the door
will be opened.

Matthew 7:7–8

Either God is not powerful enough or God is not good enough. Either way, it felt like the only choice I was left with was to diminish my view of God."

Jenna wasn't looking directly at me when she said it. She was looking off in the distance. Maybe because it was hard to look me in the eye through the emotion, or maybe because it wasn't me she was saying it to. Maybe she was saying it to God, and I was unintentionally eavesdropping. We sat across a single desk in a cramped office in a coworking space in Brooklyn as she told me the most personal version of a story I had watched her live these past seven years.

Theologians call the unavoidable question that enters our lives because of suffering "theodicy," an English word formed from two Latin words that mean "justice of God." There is no spirituality, philosophy, or worldview that manages to sidestep the theodicy riddle. No matter how you explain life, you're stuck trying to fit the square peg called "justice" into the round hole called "suffering."

Jesus fell to his knees in Gethsemane just hours before his arrest and crucifixion, and a prayer spilled out of his anguished soul: "*Abba*, Father, everything is possible for you."[1] It's a beautiful sentiment, holding in tension the approachability and majesty of God. In the same breath, Jesus calls God *Abba* and acknowledges his limitless power. The intimate Father is also the One for whom nothing is out of reach.

"*Abba*, Father, everything is possible for you." And there's the rub. If that's true, then God has got some explaining to do. Because—at least from my vantage point, and I imagine from yours too—there's a long, egregious list of things that a God who is infinite in power and perfect in love hasn't done.

They say misery loves company, but company doesn't remove the pain of misery. So it's worth pointing out that Jesus' Gethsemane prayer wasn't answered in the manner he prayed it. The cup of suffering was not taken from him. The one born without the help of biology, who moved across a lake like it was a dance floor, who fed the masses with a boy's tuna sandwich, who used dirt and spit to cure blindness, who sent demons running with their tails tucked, and who breathed life into corpses with a single command also endured the silence of God. Unanswered prayer stalks Jesus' final twenty-four hours.

As I waited silently on my side of the desk, Jenna eventually broke the silence. "You go your whole life just assuming you'll decide one day you want to have kids, and that's when you'll have them. One day, 'we're ready,' and then you flip to the next chapter," Jenna said. "But it didn't work that way for us."

Jenna is a woman of prayer. She believes in a God who hears and responds. No, it's more than that; she *expects* God's response, depends on it.

She and her husband, Liam, were penniless, and her survival strategy was prayer. When food was short, she prayed for groceries and they received free produce, courtesy of a local church's food pantry. When they were short on rent, Jenna asked God, only to return to their apartment one evening and discover someone had slipped an anonymous check under the door for the exact amount needed.

Because they were rationing out each meal as frugally as possible, they reheated a lot of leftovers—pretty challenging, since their modest apartment had no microwave. Naturally, Jenna prayed.

Two days later, she was standing in the parking lot of a laundromat in a seedy part of town where she volunteered with an organization that cared for houseless addicts and those turning to prostitution for survival. This had been her routine for a while. Many of those she served became friends. So there she was, in the parking lot around midnight, ministering among a group of sex workers, when a car pulled up. Someone threw open the trunk and grabbed what under the dark night sky and dim streetlights looked like a heavy box. "Any of you happen to need a microwave?" And that's how she got her microwave, the very one she had prayed for forty-eight hours earlier.

A nagging question lived in the background of these frequent stories though. "God, I asked you for a microwave once, and you gave it to me. I've asked you for a baby every day for years, and all I get is silence. Why are you so in touch with the trivial needs of my life and so distant from my deepest desire?"

Couldn't we all ask that question, or at least one like it? Don't we all have at least one critical area of our lives in which God, who is present in so many ways, is conspicuously absent and excruciatingly silent?

If God responded with a straightforward no, it'd be a bitter pill, but at least we'd know God heard us and in his infinite wisdom and eternal perspective responded in the negative. "No" is disillusioning, but still leaves a foundation for ongoing communication. "No" invites further relationship. But silence? Silence feels like apathy for the sufferer, like God is unmoved and uncaring about what's going on down here.

Do any of the following statements feel familiar? *Silence makes me feel like the only One with the power to stop the disease that is ravaging my mother from the inside out can't be bothered. Or the only One with the power to open my stubborn womb is too distracted to care. Or the One I've held my desire for companionship in front of for decades yawns in the face of my loneliness.* Silence means God sees and hears but is willfully ignoring my distress. That's what divine silence *feels like* to the praying person with their hands clasped.

Around the same time, Jenna's sister-in-law, Helen, was diagnosed with cervical cancer. A tumor was discovered that was quietly growing in this healthy young woman, who was only in her twenties. It was a diagnosis that could be treated, but the treatment would make it next to impossible to carry a child to full-term. Helen and Jenna became close quickly because they were living through the quiet grief of infertility side by side.

Through fervent prayer, Jenna felt certain that, against all the medical odds, God would give Will and Helen a baby. Sure enough, months after her diagnosis, Helen was pregnant. Henry was born that September. Jenna recalls the celebration of the miracle among the family. And what's more, after several rounds of IVF treatment, Jenna was pregnant too. Both of these long-awaited prayers were finally answered.

Months into Henry's life, though, Helen was still in pain. She was told it would take a while to recover from C-section surgery, but things just weren't getting much better. She went in for an examination. A massive, inoperable tumor was discovered in her abdomen. The cancer had come back aggressively. It had been growing inside her long enough that it was attached to several vital organs. The doctors wouldn't be able to touch it. The tumor was hiding behind Henry. Life and death were growing in Helen's abdomen simultaneously.

Seven months of aggressive chemotherapy and radiation therapy later, there was nothing more the doctors could do. The tumor kept growing. The treatment wasn't working.

Helen turned to alternative medicine and a strict diet. This treatment was a last resort, but she was convinced something would work. "Why would God give me this miracle baby and then take his mom in the process? God is going to make a way."

That was June. By July, she had begun to deteriorate rapidly.

In August, Helen was in such bad shape that Jenna boarded a plane for Ireland, clinging to hope, praying for another miracle. That hope took a serious blow the moment she saw Helen. "I walked into the hospital room and nearly doubled over when I laid eyes on her. Immediately I thought, *Lord, I don't think you can do this. I don't think anyone comes back when they're this far gone.*"

The next day, Jenna and the others brought Helen home from hospital, not knowing that in less than a week she'd be gone. More and more family gathered. They were all there, waiting for her to go, waiting to say goodbye. No one said it out loud, but the cloud of death hung heavily over the house.

Jenna sat in the nursery, giving space to the family that had gathered by Helen's bedside—her husband, Will, along with her mother, father, and siblings.

"There's something strange that happens when you've sat for hours at the bedside of the dying," Jenna told me. "You get so used to just listening to her breathe; it's like a piece of music with a rhythm and a melody. You can hear when there's a key change. I heard it from the hallway. I knew it was time."

Jenna walked into the room and stood alongside the family. It could've been several hours or only a few minutes. Time is relative in moments like those. After a long, mournful silence, it was Jenna who spoke for all gathered at the bedside, "We don't want you to be scared, Helen. It's okay. You can go." And she did. It was less than a week before Henry's first birthday.

A few weeks later, Jenna returned to New York. "I walked into my home," Jenna explained, "and the weight of the loss finally came down on me like an anvil. The last time I set foot in this apartment, I was packing up to go, counting on a miracle. Now I'm back here. And she's gone.

"I just couldn't see how life could keep on going like normal after this. I was grieving Helen, but I was also grieving the person I was before she died," Jenna said. "I always thought I'd be one of those Christians who hits hardship and stays strong, keeps going. I know now that I'm not that person."

She continued. "I see it now. This is the moment when so many people walk away, and I actually wanted to. But two things were keeping me. First, I was tethered to Jesus because so much good was built on him too. If I were going to deny him, I couldn't just deny his absence in this moment, but I'd have to deny his presence in so many profoundly good moments. Second, I was too angry to walk away, like when you're stammering around a room in a raging argument with your spouse and you're too angry to step outside and get some air. You've got something to say, and you've just gotta say it."

Jenna stepped back into that Brooklyn apartment, a landmark of faith in a God who heals. God could've healed Helen, could've given her thousands of days with the husband she loved, could've given her the joy of watching little Henry grow up, and could've given her husband and son the gift of watching her grow old. But God didn't give any of that.

"*Abba*, Father, everything is possible for you." And if Jesus was right about that, then God either willed something so painful that it seems unforgivable or maybe God didn't will Helen's death but just allowed it. That lands a bit softer, but does it make God any less culpable? God may not be a murderer, but doesn't that make him a doctor who has the cure to cancer buried in the drawer of his nightstand, and yet he's just sitting at home flipping through channels while people die of the disease he knows how to heal? "*Abba*, Father, everything is possible for you." How can that be?

I've had the experience of praying for someone in a hospital room whom the medical staff had left for dead, only to see that person wake up and go on living. I've experienced the euphoria of the moments following such an event, the supernatural joy that floods the grieving—the heaven-kissing-earth sort of wonder at a God who intervenes.

I've also held the hand of a young man in a drug-induced coma—his wife, son, parents, and siblings all in the waiting room—desperately hoping God will listen to my prayers because he doesn't seem to be listening to theirs. I've anointed that man's head with oil, prayed for his life, and walked out of that hospital room an hour later past the grieving family who was coming to terms with the fact that he wasn't coming back, my prayers no more obviously helpful than their own.

I know the power of God and the silence of God, and sometimes I think I'd handle the silence better if power was never on the table at all. A God with a personality and a will is so unpredictable. Maybe it would be easier if we had a God who worked like an operating system designed to deliver predictable results based on the buttons I push. But that's not the God revealed on the pages of

Scripture. It's not the God revealed in Jesus. It's not the God I've walked with all these years.

The Deeper Invitation

Of everything that Jesus had to say on the subject of prayer, there are perhaps no more famous or confusing words than the three simple verbs—*ask*, *seek*, and *knock*—he uses in the Sermon on the Mount in Matthew 7. On the one hand, they issue an empowering and straightforward invitation, and on the other hand, this invitation doesn't deliver consistent, predictable results. Was this false advertising? Did Jesus overpromise? Or is his original meaning lost in translation across centuries, traditions, and translations?

In these three verbs, Jesus is naming the trail markers on the common prayer journey, a path tread by men and women of faith stretching all the way back to the beginning. Prayer is a journey that starts with need and ends in relationship. When we are born into this world, our first words are unintelligible cries of pain and need. Babies weep and wail before they learn coherent speech, before they learn relational trust in the mother and father who brought them into this world. Likewise, prayer is primal language, instinctively emerging from us in the face of pain and suffering. Need first drives us to our knees, but relationship keeps us there. That's what Jesus was getting at—the deeper invitation hidden in three simple verbs—*ask*, *seek*, and *knock*.

Ask refers to the requests that bring us to prayer. Most prayers are preceded by need—a diagnosis, a car accident, yet another negative pregnancy test, a holiday with the absence of a loved one, another week without a call back on a single application, a credit card bill that keeps climbing, a breakup, a divorce. Life has a way of dealing us a card or two we never saw coming and don't know how to make sense of. We are happily humming along, content with our fragile, elusive sense of control over our lives when all of a sudden we are gut-punched, mugged in broad daylight, and robbed of the life we thought was so securely "ours." When we find ourselves in a story we don't recognize, with no way back to the plot we thought we were living, we pray. We "ask."

Seek is a word peppered throughout Scripture that often refers to God himself. We are instructed to seek God through the stories of kings and judges, the poetry of the psalms, and the cries of the prophets. By using the word *seek*, Jesus pointed the way along the path of prayer: we come asking and discover relationship amid the mess. We come seeking gifts, and we often get them! But the greatest gift, the One we're really after and the One we're guaranteed to receive, is the Giver himself.

Knock, Jesus' final verb in this teaching on prayer in the Sermon on the Mount, is the destination of the prayer journey that begins in need. Biblically speaking, *knock* prompts the imagery of table fellowship.

This is a provocative image in today's world of fast food, power lunches, and takeout dinners, but it was all the more provocative in the ancient Hebrew world, where acceptance, dignity, and equality were given by table fellowship. To dine with someone back then was not merely to tolerate their company while getting some much-needed nourishment. To share a table was the greatest affirmation of their character and the truest and deepest form of intimacy.

Jesus was criticized, on multiple occasions, for breaking bread with tax collectors, prostitutes, and notorious sinners for this very reason. It was one thing for a rabbi to be seen in conversation with such a person on the street, but to share a table with them? That was unthinkable. The greatest illustration of prayer Jesus gave is the one he lived—the Infinite Other, the Alpha and Omega, the Holy and Infallible, welcomes us to his table. He does not simply tolerate our company or benevolently entertain our requests; he affirms our person, chooses our company, and delights in our presence.

"Prayer enlarges the heart until it is capable of containing God's gift of himself. Ask and seek, and your heart will grow big enough to receive him and keep him as your own," writes Mother Teresa.[2]

We come for gifts, and we get the Giver. And we find ourselves

Isogood_patrick/Shutterstock.com

seated at his table, welcomed, accepted, and loved, being fed, being listened to, relaxing in the warm presence of the loving God.

One of the most famous icons in church history, traced back to Russian painter Andrei Rublev in the fifteenth century, is commonly referred to as *The Trinity*.

It has stood the test of time because it so vividly captures the divine in a common scene—Father, Son, and Holy Spirit seated at a table, enjoying each other's company. Here we have a communal God engaged in a conversation that moves effortlessly from small talk to depth. Prayer—in any form, by anybody—is God's invitation to pull up a chair to the table and enjoy restful, intimate, unbroken conversation with the triune God. Or as Jesus succinctly said it, "Knock and the door will be opened to you."[3]

The Woman Who Wouldn't Take "No" for an Answer

Jesus told a story about prayer in the face of waiting and silence, recorded in Luke's gospel:

> Then Jesus told his disciples a parable to show them that they should always pray and not give up. He said: "In a certain town there was a judge who neither feared God nor cared what people thought. And there was a widow in that town who kept coming to him with the plea, 'Grant me justice against my adversary.'
>
> "For some time he refused. But finally he said to himself, 'Even though I don't fear God or care what people think, yet because this widow keeps bothering me, I will see that she gets justice, so that she won't eventually come and attack me!'"
>
> And the Lord said, "Listen to what the unjust judge says. And will not God bring about justice for his chosen ones, who

cry out to him day and night? Will he keep putting them off? I tell you, he will see that they get justice, and quickly."[4]

Jesus' telling of the story of a widow advocating for herself in a court was confrontational to some in his audience and ennobling to others. At this time in history, tragically, a woman's testimony was not permitted in a court of law. The place of women in society was so low that their word was not considered trustworthy in matters of justice. Among the degraded female class, widows occupied the lowest rank. Widows were not permitted to work in the Greco-Roman world, making them permanently dependent on society's charity—welfare at best, homelessness more commonly.

When Jesus told a story of praying for justice, he gave a starring role to one of the lowest members of society, one whose voice was notably silenced, the least authoritative. In Jesus' story, the woman's plea—"Grant me justice against my adversary"—was heard and granted. Persistence was required, but her request wasn't just granted; it was granted "quickly." In his choice of characters, Jesus told those who feel powerless in prayer that their prayers provoke God's action, even his quick, decisive action.

Keep On Asking

Of course, some of you are already thinking, *Yeah, man, that all sounds quite poetic, but what about the other side of the coin—what about when our asking doesn't result in receiving, our seeking leaves us with more questions than answers, and despite our knocking, this door just isn't opening? What about when the events of life lead us to prayer, but our prayer leaves us there alone, in the same place?*

These three words—*ask, seek,* and *knock*—are written in a Greek verb tense we don't have a grammatical equivalent for in English.

It implies not a single action but an ongoing action, one that takes place in the present *and* into the future. The most literal translation of Matthew 7:7 is, "Keep on asking and you will receive; keep on seeking and you will find; keep on knocking and the door will be opened to you." In fact, many English translations translate it that way, word for word.[5]

What is Jesus' response to those of us who find ourselves asking without receiving an answer, seeking without finding, knocking without being welcomed in? How does Jesus respond to the real, deep questions of those praying faithfully, waiting patiently, and beginning to grow weary?

Persistence. "Keep on asking, keep on seeking, keep on knocking." It's an unsatisfying response. Depending on your specific story of waiting and silence, it may even be insensitive and offensive.

Jesus knew this would be a hard pill to swallow, so he told several stories to illustrate the point, to put flesh and bones on it, to ground it not in the theoretical world of stained-glass buildings and homilies but in the gritty, down-to-earth world of real life. My favorite is the story of the stubborn widow who pleaded her case relentlessly before the stingy judge. It serves as the biblical ground zero for those who, in response to the waiting that prayer entails, have lowered their expectations about God, watered down Jesus' blunt "ask, seek, knock" declaration into some good but lesser version that allows them to hold on to the God they love without being disappointed or angered by the ways that God seems to be failing them.

Jesus had a motive in telling this particular story. It's distinct in that the moral of the story is given up front. Normally, the meanings of Jesus' parables are kept mysterious, but here Luke steals the punch line. "Then Jesus told his disciples a parable to show them that they should always pray and not give up."[6] Luke knows it'll be hard to hear this, see this, understand this. He, like

Jesus, knows that persistence can be hard to stomach, so he comes right out and says it: "Jesus painted a picture for you to hold on to like a life raft when you're drowning in silence and disappointment. Here it comes."

The promise of the story is found in its most dynamic character—the slimy judge. "For some time he refused. But finally he said to himself, 'Even though I don't fear God or care what people think, yet because this widow keeps bothering me, I will see that she gets justice, so that she won't eventually come and attack me!'"[7]

If Jesus compares the person at prayer to the persistent widow, is he also comparing God to the judge? That doesn't seem like a flattering mirror to hold up to God. He's reluctant, self-interested, annoyed, and weak. But Jesus interprets his own parable for us: "And the Lord said, 'Listen to what the unjust judge says. And will not God bring about justice for his chosen ones, who cry out to him day and night? Will he keep putting them off? I tell you, he will see that they get justice, and quickly.'"[8]

Jesus doesn't compare the unjust judge to God. He distinguishes God from the judge. His point is that "if even a judge this bad will give justice to the persistent, how much more will God see that those persistent in prayer get justice?" "Prayer is not begging God to do something for us that he doesn't know about, or begging God to do something for us that he is reluctant to do, or begging God to do something that he hasn't time for," writes Eugene Peterson. "In prayer we persistently, faithfully, trustingly come before God, submitting ourselves to his sovereignty, confident that he is acting, right now, on our behalf."[9] Where does this confidence come from? From the assurance that we are his "chosen ones," as Jesus names us in the same breath. What's God up to right now? He's weaving history into a redemptive, good future for his chosen ones—that's you, me, and all who call Jesus "Lord."

Prayers and Tears

Scripture makes it clear that God collects two things—prayers and tears. This world in its current form is passing away, but our prayers and tears are eternal.

God collects our prayers. In Revelation, we are offered a glimpse at the receiving end of our prayers: "The twenty-four elders fell down before the Lamb. Each one had a harp and they were holding golden bowls full of incense, which are the prayers of God's people."[10] Do you realize what that means? It means every prayer you've ever whispered, from the simplest throwaway request to the most heartfelt cry, God has collected it like a grandmother who scrapbooks a toddler's finger paints and scribbles. God has treasured up every prayer we've ever uttered, even the ones we've forgotten, and he's still weaving their fulfillment, bending history in the direction of a great *yes* to you and me.

John's Revelation doesn't end with God as a scrapbooking grandmother though; it ends with God as a powerful Redeemer. Three chapters later, those heavenly golden prayer bowls reappeared:

> Another angel, who had a golden censer, came and stood at the altar. He was given much incense to offer, with the prayers of all God's people, on the golden altar in front of the throne. The smoke of the incense, together with the prayers of God's people, went up before God from the angel's hand. Then the angel took the censer, filled it with fire from the altar, and hurled it on the earth; and there came peals of thunder, rumblings, flashes of lightning and an earthquake.[11]

At the proper time, God is tipping the bowl, pouring out our requests on the earth. He has collected every prayer we've ever prayed, and redemption comes when he rains down those prayers on the earth once and for all. The renewal of the world, heaven and earth restored as one, begins with God pouring out all the prayers of his children like a purifying fire with one great, resounding *yes*. Every prayer in the end is an answered prayer. Some are still awaiting that yes, but it's coming. That's the kind of "judge" we're dealing with.

God collects more than just the words wedged between "Dear God" and "Amen" though. He also collects our tears. Psalm 56 reads, "You have kept count of my tossings; put my tears in your bottle. Are they not in your book?"[12]

Prayer is asking, looking from the vantage point of heaven and pointing God into the mess. But prayer is also weeping—in the middle of a mess so thick we can't see up, but can only scream through tears, "Lord, I can't bear it any longer!"

The psalmist tells us in Psalm 126:5, "Those who sow with tears will reap with songs of joy." Not only will God collect every tear, but he'll redeem every tear. God is not merely bottling up our tears. He also promises that when they touch the earth, they will bring renewal. Every tear of ours that falls to the ground will grow the fruit of redemption. God bends history so that the moments of greatest pain become the moments of greatest redemption, twisting the story to be sure that the pain we feel releases the power of new life, and the tears we cry become the foundation of a better world. We are promised that a day is coming when the Father himself will wipe away every tear from our eyes. But until then, we live on an in-between promise: "I will not let a single one of your tears be wasted."[13]

So here is the promise revealed to the persistent widow, spoken to us by our faithful Father: "I hear you, and I will make all things right, all things new." That new creation is seeded by the prayers of God's people and watered by their tears. Both are key ingredients in the remaking of the world.

Our persistence in prayer comes from the promise that we don't pray to a reluctant, half-interested, can't-be-bothered judge, but to an unfathomably loving Father who collects our prayers like love letters and our tears like fine wine.

The final word Jesus speaks in the parable doesn't come in the form of a promise but a challenge: "I tell you, [God] will see that they get justice, and quickly. However, when the Son of Man comes, will he find faith on the earth?"[14] In the story, even Jesus admits that most people lose steam in the long journey of asking, seeking, and knocking. He promises a good ending, so good in fact that it'll redeem not just the distorted creation as a whole but every moment of suffering from every individual life—none of it will have been wasted. But Jesus asks us, "When the time for that full and final redemption comes, will I find men and women of faith? Will I find any who haven't lost heart along the way? Any who have trusted me and my promise enough to keep praying in the face of waiting and disappointment?" Will he find us hollowed and flattened by our spiritual disappointment, or awake and hopeful even as we confront the unjust state of a darkened world? Will he find in us the persistent prayer of the widow who cried out day and night?

When we've grown impatient with the waiting, lost our stamina for persistence, what keeps us praying? We must recover an understanding of the way God is at work, not just in the final promise, but in all the acts of persistence along the way.

Choosing Trust

Jenna sat in her grief counselor's office. She was at her weekly appointment, trying to sift through the mess that unanswered prayer had dumped in her lap. It was a question, not an answer, that served as her subtle hinge point between the pain that destroys and the pain that transforms. The counselor gently asked her, "What reason could God give you? What I mean is, what could God say to you, Jenna, that would justify Helen's death? Is there any reason he could offer for not healing her that you would find satisfactory, any answer that would make her loss okay?"

"And the truth is," Jenna spoke slowly, reverently, to me now—as if we were in an ornate chapel rather than a bustling office, and as if returning to the memory of that day in the counselor's office was to step onto holy ground—"the truth is there was nothing. And that realization left me with a choice to make. I could embrace mystery or run from it. Could I make peace with not knowing why my prayers weren't answered, or would this be the experience I define God by, the one experience that overwhelms all the others I'd had along the way? Could I continue to trust God without having answers and reasons? We are all going to face painful disorientation at some point, and the challenging invitation is to trust even in the darkness."

Wrestling with God through persistent prayer is a confirmation of true belief, not distressing doubt. Those who only half-heartedly believe don't take offense at silence. It is only those of us who believe and believe hard—hard enough to walk out on a limb of faith with our full weight, who feel that limb snap beneath us and send us into a free fall without a harness, who care to wrestle with a God who at times seems fickle—it is only those who are offended by silence.

Jenna went on. Her tea had run cold, and both of us were now tearfully quiet. "Pain and suffering have the capacity to deepen you and transform you, but they also have the capacity to destroy you. I realized that this pain I carried was destroying me."

Will the pain, suffering, and needs that intrude on our own stories harden our hearts, or will they soften our souls? How does the very pain that is eating us alive become an agent of deep transformation? We have to invite God—the very One who broke our trust—into the muck with us. We invite the One we are labeling "perpetrator" to be our healer. It's the most courageous of all choices.

Jenna continued. "As a young Christian, my faith was built on the resurrection power of Jesus. The God who drew me into the story and led me to this point in the journey was the victorious Savior. Now I got to know the suffering servant and the man of sorrows.[15] The very spiritual life that first bloomed as I danced around God's throne now kept growing as I, like Thomas, ran my fingers over Jesus' wounds."

There, feeling her way around in the dark, it wasn't a God of resurrection power she discovered, but a God willing to enter the night and feel around in that same darkness with her. A God weeping in the garden. A God hanging on a cross. A suffering servant. A man of sorrows.

Jesus reveals a God who is offensively human, in contrast to any other world religion. A God who knows the overwhelming nature of suffering in a fallen world. A God who miraculously healed a leper, only to go on living in a world filled with leper colonies, who opened the eyes of a blind man on the same day another baby was born blind. A God who displays healing power and also chooses personal suffering as the means to final healing.

Jenna discovered there, quite personally, the truth named by Parker Palmer: "The deeper our faith, the more doubt we must endure; the deeper our hope, the more prone we are to despair; the deeper our love, the more pain its loss will bring: these are a few of the paradoxes we must hold as human beings. If we refuse to hold them in the hopes of living without doubt, despair, and pain, we also find ourselves living without hope, faith, and love."[16]

When Jenna stepped back into her apartment after Helen's death, the story she had built her life on came tumbling down like a house of cards. The way she described it then was like this: "Either God is not powerful enough or God is not good enough." Months later, after wandering in the dark, seething in the church pew, grieving the loss of a version of herself she missed and couldn't get back to, another option finally opened to her.

"In that grief counselor's office that day, I made my decision. I chose trust. Not a trust that God willed Helen's cancer or death, but a trust that God is good, that God is present in our suffering, and that God will make all things new." Jenna and I both sat in silence with tearstained faces. Somehow the tiny office in that bustling coworking space had become as holy as the most ornate chapel.

I don't (and never could) understand everything about God. But I can trust the God who is revealed in Jesus—the God who has never looked down on suffering from a lofty throne but has always looked into the eyes of the suffering from level ground. I can trust the God who refuses to offer platitudes from a safe distance, the God who descends into the mess with me.

All the biblical highlights, the moments of God's glorious interventions, were preceded by someone choosing trust. The subtext behind every miracle, the soundtrack beneath the life of every saint, is a defiant and courageous choice in the face of the dark experience of God's absence and silence: "I choose trust."

C. S. Lewis names this choice as the great defiance from which redemption springs: "Our [Satan and his minions] cause is never more in danger than when a human, no longer desiring, but still intending, to do our Enemy's will, looks round upon a universe from which every trace of Him seems to have vanished, and asks why he has been forsaken, and still obeys."[17]

An Execution and a Rescue

Acts 12 tells the incredible story of Peter's supernatural deliverance from prison. He gets thrown into jail for his faith in Jesus, has a public execution date set for the next day. Meanwhile, the church gathers at somebody's house, holds an all-night prayer meeting, and in the wee hours of the morning, Peter shows up at that very prayer meeting.

As it turned out, God was listening and doing the miraculous. He opened a locked cell in the middle of the night and guided Peter from shackles to freedom so he could rejoin the church family that had been asking on his behalf.

That's the headline. It's the story everyone remembers from Acts 12, and it's a good one. But I'm not interested in the headline; I'm caught up in the subtext:

> It was about this time that King Herod arrested some who belonged to the church, intending to persecute them. He had James, the brother of John, put to death with the sword. When he saw that this met with approval among the Jews, he proceeded to seize Peter also. (Acts 12:1–3)

God miraculously freed Peter, but James was unjustly executed. Why? Why did God respond miraculously to prayer for Peter, but silently to prayer for James? Both of these men were in his inner, inner circle, his core three disciples, so it wasn't that he favored one over the other. Surely the church prayed for both. If they gathered for an all-night prayer meeting for Peter, it's safe to assume they responded in the same way for James. Both were arrested and imprisoned by the same corrupt tyrant for the same unjust cause, perhaps even occupied the same jail cell. So, why God? Why let James die if you have the power to teleport Peter to safety?

I don't know. That's the only honest response.

Here's what I do know: God works slowly out of compassion, not apathy. I know God puts up with a ton of corruption, and his slow, loving way of redemption asks of us patience and endurance in suffering. I know that when I read Acts, I see a seasoned, resilient faith—a praying people who dance with God through miracles and bear with God through mystery.

Lost in the background of the action sequences and miraculous montages of Acts is this—a community that gathered to pray, even after they had tried it once before only to watch darkness win, at least from their point of view. They kept on praying in the face of unanswered prayer. They persisted in prayer.

Where does that come from? Only from the belief that God is bottling up my tears and saving them right next to my prayers. That both are key ingredients in the recipe of redemption. That he loves me too much to let either go to waste.

Can we become again a persistently praying kind of people? Can we recover the legacy of our ancient ancestors, lost somewhere along the way? Can we preserve it, enflesh it in our bodies, express it in our lives?

"Keep on asking and it will be given to you. Keep on seeking and you will find. Keep on knocking and the door will be opened to you." That's the invitation Jesus offered us. And anyone who takes him up on it and prays this way long enough will eventually find themselves on the doorstep of resilience.

PRACTICE

Persistent Prayer

Prayer in the form of the persistent widow can be understood in three movements.

1. Say It Like You Mean It

Don't begin with grit or faith. Start with disappointment, naming your pain and need to God. He collects our tears, and we begin by doing the same, dragging up our painful experiences of his perceived absence, silence, or rejection. Tell God your disappointments in prayer, and don't water it down. Forget your manners. Tell it like it is.

2. Listen for the Question

Invite God to show you the question beneath your disappointments. You'll know you're at the root when you get to a deeper question. Beneath the circumstances left in the wake of your disappointment lives a question about the character of God. Is God really loving? Is God really listening? Does God really care about *this* part of my life? Is God really powerful? Can God heal even this? Is God really bending all toward redemption? Remember, there's a question hooked into God's person, his character. Listen till you find it.

3. Ask God to Meet You in the Question

Hold your deep question before God, inviting him to bring healing. He heals through this process of pointed questions, so this question you've discovered holds within it the power of healing. Invite him and keep inviting. He's a miracle-working God who sometimes opens the eyes of the blind. He's also a divine companion who sometimes stumbles around with us in the dark, wearing our pain alongside us. He's a master healer. Our only role is to invite and keep inviting.

It is through this process that you will discover the faith to ask again, to keep on interceding, to fill up that heavenly bowl. He is less interested in our asking out of duty or gritted teeth and more interested in the kind of asking that emerges from the healed heart of recovered faith.

Chapter 10

REBELLIOUS FIDELITY

Unceasing Prayer

Pray without ceasing.
1 Thessalonians 5:17 ESV

He tears her out of her bed and marches her, with a fistful of hair knotted up in his clenched right fist, to the town square, where he throws her down in front of the temple steps. The whole place falls silent. A woman is lying facedown in the dirt at the rabbi's feet.[1]

A few minutes ago, the adulterous woman was entangled in the web of a double life. The affair picked up where she had left it the day before—only today, the thrill of infidelity was interrupted by the presence of an unwanted third. A priest had walked in on them. Caught them in the act.

The same priest who created the moment of disgrace also broke the silence. "The Law says death penalty. Stone her. What do you say?" He was forcing the self-proclaimed rabbi to take a stand between the people and the Law. It was a brilliant equation, the perfect trap. The woman was lying there, wrapped in nothing but the thin top sheet from her lover's bed, cheek pressed against the dirt. The carefree thrill of a few minutes ago had been replaced by the heavy weight of shame that was pinning her to the ground.

Her mind races. *How long have they known, and who else knows? It's almost time to pick up the kids. Someone will tell them, or worse, they'll bring them here. They'll let them see me like this. They'll make them watch as some kind of warning. And what does it feel like when they actually stone you?*

Jesus doesn't respond to the priest's question. He stoops down and starts drawing in the dirt. She's close enough to hear the scraping sound of his index finger running through the sand as the onlookers lean in to try to make out what he's writing.

Just when the silence has hung long enough that the priest is about to blurt out something else, Jesus speaks up. "Alright, go ahead and stone her. But whoever is without sin must throw the first rock."

She flinches when she hears the first sound, but then she realizes, *They're not throwing their stones. They're dropping them.*

She raises her head to meet his eyes of compassion. "Neither do I condemn you," Jesus declares. "Go now and leave your life of sin."[2]

This is the story she would've gone on telling forever. Her place of great shame became the place of great mercy. The very part of her story she wanted to erase or hide in the fine print at the bottom of the page became the very part of her story she'd never stop telling. That's the kind of author God is. He doesn't edit. He repurposes and redeems. He turns the worst moments into the irreplaceable, climactic ones. Her most obvious failure was also her greatest victory.

But what would've been impossible for this woman to know, still stunned by the sudden intrusion of love, is that the real fight of her life had just begun. The real fight takes place every day after this transcendent, memorable day.

We've all got a "woman caught in adultery" moment or two

in our past that profoundly reshaped us, but when it comes to the many days after that passionate encounter (the fidelity), we typically find those to be underwhelming and disenchanting.

There are highs and lows in the spiritual life—supernatural encounters, fiery passion, and healing forgiveness; loneliness, grief, and existential crises. But the most common condition found in the pew at your local house of worship is a general malaise of boredom.

The exhilaration of our mountaintop experiences wears thin after a while, and we find ourselves reluctantly dragging our feet along the narrow path behind Jesus, yawning all the way. But spiritual boredom isn't necessarily a sign that we're lapsing in prayer; in fact, it often means we're maturing.

The real fight of faith comes on all the ordinary days after the climactic moment because of what we all know but are too polite to come right out and admit: fidelity is boring.

Prayer Is about Love

The Bible is not a rule book or a set of directions; it's a love story—a romantic, courageous love story we're invited to believe. We see that whole story captured in a single scene when Jesus defends and dignifies a shame-covered woman thrown into the dirt at his feet, but we can see it just as clearly when we zoom all the way out to the metanarrative that God has been authoring since hanging the stars in the night sky.

The biblical story begins with perfect love at the center of the plot, and the conflict introduced by sin is a twisting and warping of that love into something lesser. The hinge point at the story's center is the life, death, and resurrection of Jesus. The wound opened up by infidelity is mended by a love that will never give up. Jesus, on the final night of his life, says this to his followers: "As the Father has loved me, so have I loved you. Now remain in my love."[3] The whole sixty-six-book anthology becomes resolved, not in a catastrophic apocalypse, but at a wedding banquet—Christ united to his bride for all eternity.[4] Human infidelity repaired by divine fidelity.

How do we remain in that love? How do we make covenant love the constant backdrop before which the scenes of our lives play out? Prayer. "If you can't love, you can't pray, either," writes Johannes Hartl. "Praying is loving. And learning to pray means learning to love."[5]

Love is easy at the first and at the last. It's effortless in the honeymoon stage when you're infatuated with each other—touchy, talkative, and smitten. And love is like breathing for the old couple who are decades into a mature love that has been aged to perfection like a fine wine. But all those years in between? Love in the midst of building a career, raising kids, establishing a life, and facing trials—those are the long years when love has to be worked at and fought for. Those are the years when early infatuation is matured into the old couple in effortless union. Those are the years when love is won and lost.

Like love, prayer comes easy at the first and at the last, for sinners and saints, but all the years in between are the important ones. Prayer is about relationship, and that means fidelity is the only container within which it can truly flourish.

When I was seventeen years old, a senior in high school, a waterfront park lay right along my commute home from school. Regularly, multiple times a week, I'd stop there on the way home and walk the shaded paths of that park in unhurried, agenda-free conversation with God.

I've got stories of prayer walking with a mission, seeing sparks of revival in the early mornings at a public middle school. I know the prayer of intensity and fire. I also know the prayer of fidelity and love. On those afternoons at Philippe Park, I did not want anything from God. I had no plans I wanted him to sponsor, no needs I was hoping he'd meet. There was no motive; there was only love. I wanted to be with God, so I walked and talked and listened.

A couple decades removed, I now imagine those afternoons were God's favorites. There's no way to know for sure, but I have a sneaking suspicion he preferred those meandering afternoon strolls to the early mornings with a school directory in hand and a vision in mind. Because on those weekday afternoons, it wasn't about changing the world. It wasn't about getting God to act the way I thought God should act. It wasn't even about my own issues or needs. There was no function. We "waste" time with those we love. And I was stealing time with God because I love him.

"Prayer does not mean much when we undertake it only as an attempt to influence God, or as a search for a spiritual fallout shelter, or as an offering of comfort in stress-filled times," writes Henri Nouwen. "Prayer is the act by which we divest ourselves of all false belongings and become free to belong to God and God alone."[6]

Before prayer is about power or outcomes or heavenly armies and a righteous uprising, it's about love. It's the way we freely choose the God who freely chose us first. The way we express ourselves to the God who, in spite of everything, delights in us. The way we receive from the God who has endless stamina to offer himself to a bunch of people who prefer self-sufficiency, tight jaws, and clenched fists.

The Heart of a Lover and the Discipline of a Monk

"Teach us to pray."[7] That's the request we keep returning to. Prayer is what people noticed about Jesus more than anything else. Prayer is the aspect of his life those who got close to him were most jealous for.

Watching Jesus pray was like watching the closing scene from the movie *The Notebook*. You know the one. After the twists and turns of young, passionate, infatuated love, Ryan Gosling and Rachel McAdams have wrinkled and plumped into any other hobbling, elderly couple. They're in a hospital room, both nearing the end. He lies down in her bed, wraps his arm around her, interlaces his fingers with hers, and they fall asleep for good, together. Dying, but still in love, still holding on to each other.

Everyone who has ever watched that movie gets at least a little misty-eyed during that scene because it meets us at the place of our God-given longing. We all want that intimacy and companionship. Everyone wants that, but there's a reason the writer and director of *The Notebook* included only the honeymoon stage and the mature love in the end. It's the most obvious reason: all those years in between are filled with nothing but ordinary fidelity. And fidelity is boring.

When you see the fruit of fidelity though—an elderly couple still in love—a thought runs through every mind: *That's better than anything I've got. I want that.* That's what the disciples saw when Jesus prayed—the fruit of fidelity. And they wanted it. "Teach us the kind of prayer that leads to that."

"Our Father in heaven, hallowed be your name, your kingdom come, your will be done, on earth as it is in heaven."[8] In his exemplary prayer, Jesus was up to something obvious to the twelve but lost on modern disciples. The Lord's Prayer was not entirely original to Jesus. It wasn't something he was rattling off spontaneously.

Jesus was adapting the opening lines of the Kaddish, one of the three esteemed, familiar prayers recited regularly in the ancient

The Kaddish	The Lord's Prayer
Magnified and sanctified may His great name be,	Our Father in heaven, hallowed be your name,
in the world He created by his will. May He establish His kingdom in your lifetime and in your days.	your kingdom come, your will be done, on earth as it is in heaven.

Jewish temple. It reads, "Magnified and sanctified may His great name be, in the world He created by His will. May He establish His kingdom in your lifetime and in your days."[9]

Take a look, side by side:[10]

I'm not trying to accuse Jesus of anything immoral here, but that's definitely plagiarism in college. Jesus is adapting a common, disciplined Hebrew prayer from the temple, and making it much, much, much more personal for personal people in search of a personal God.

"Teach us to pray." And Jesus responds, essentially, "Pray to God more intimately than you think you're allowed to because this is about love, *and* center your life according to a disciplined rhythm of prayer because fidelity is the soil that love grows in." I hear Jesus saying, "Here's my secret: pray with the heart of a lover and the discipline of a monk. That's how you choose fidelity, and when you do, it quenches your desires in such a satisfying way that everything else becomes the boring part." Jesus was saying to them and to us, "Pray like a bunch of wild, unruly monks."

Dietrich Bonhoeffer once offered a famous piece of advice to a young couple on their wedding day: "Today, you are young and very much in love and you think that your love can sustain your marriage. It can't. Let your marriage sustain your love."[11] Prayer is about love, and that means it cannot be sustained on fluttery feelings, good intentions, and spontaneous moments alone. It needs a container, something like the fidelity of a marriage, a set of practices or rituals within which that love can grow, mature, and blossom.

"To have lived as a one and then suddenly become a two—that is an invasion," writes *New York Times* columnist David Brooks. "And yet there is a prize. People in long, happy marriages have won the lottery of life . . . Passion peaks among the young, but marriage is the thing that peaks in old age."[12] And just as old couples grow more like each other through years of companionship, we grow more like Jesus over hours of conversation, years of companionship.

This idea is neither new nor novel. Woven through various traditions and eras from modern church history all the way back to the church's inception, a set rhythm of prayer has grounded the relationship between God and his people.

Pray Like a Monk

The way to pray like Jesus taught us to pray includes this unavoidable invitation: learn to live like a monk in the ordinary world. Historically speaking, this is the drum that God's people have always been beating.

In the Hebrew tradition, which contains the very roots of the Christian faith, there has always been a daily prayer rhythm: pausing to pray three times a day—morning, midday, and evening. In fact, all the great spiritual traditions insist on some kind of a daily prayer rhythm.[13] This is the central plot point of the book of Daniel. He refuses to renounce prayer to Yahweh in a Babylonian culture.

He won't stop kneeling to pray three times a day in front of his Jerusalem-facing window. He lives by a daily prayer rhythm, and he will not order his prayer life according to the culture, customs, and expectations of that foreign land. That's the offense that gets him thrown to the lions.

Likewise, the psalmist unites the voice of all God's people: "As for me, I call to God, and the LORD saves me. Evening, morning and noon I cry out in distress, and he hears my voice."[14]

Jesus himself observed a daily prayer rhythm. Every one of the Gospels contains descriptions of Jesus withdrawing from his activity for set times of prayer. There are seventeen scenes of Jesus at prayer.

It's important to note that not every reference to Jesus in prayer was planned according to a fixed, daily rhythm. It wasn't temple custom to stay up all night on a moonlit prayer hike, for instance, so Jesus did pray spontaneously. But it's equally important to note that Jesus did pray according to a fixed, daily rhythm. The overwhelming historic evidence is that Jesus prayed according to the temple rhythm—three times a day—observing the same morning, midday, and evening rhythm we see in Daniel and the Psalms. In fact, many of the biblical references to Jesus in prayer fall into that category.[15] New Testament theologian Scot McKnight summarizes, "Jesus prayed within the sacred rhythms of Israel, and he knew firsthand their formative influence."[16] Jesus prayed spontaneously *and* routinely, alone *and* with others, pouring out his emotions in his own words *and* guided by the psalms at fixed hours in the temple. Jesus prayed like a wild, unruly monk.

The early church, whose shared life we've been trying to recapture for about seventeen hundred years now, lived by a daily prayer rhythm. In Acts, the apostles picked up exactly where their rabbi had left off, praying like Jesus taught them.

One day Peter and John were going up to the temple at the time of prayer—at three in the afternoon. (Acts 3:1)

On their release, Peter and John went back to their own people and reported all that the chief priests and the elders had said to them. When they heard this, they raised their voices together in prayer to God. (Acts 4:23–24)

About noon the following day as they were on their journey and approaching the city, Peter went up on the roof to pray. (Acts 10:9)

The earliest nonbiblical document we have from church life is called the Didache, which, among other things, details the morning, midday, and evening prayers observed by all Christians in the early church.[17]

Have you ever wondered how the apostles were able to gather their scattered congregations for emergency prayer meetings in a huge city in a world before cell phones? The most likely explanation is that they were already gathering for prayer at set points throughout the day.

A shared, daily prayer rhythm was the assumption in the church for centuries, and then the Roman Empire fell. When that happened, the church, for the first time in its history, buddied up with political power and lost its saltiness, as Jesus put it.[18] At that same time, they lost a taste for prayer.

The first monasteries were founded in the fourth and fifth centuries simply to continue the common life of the early church. Linking arms with power, church life had become diluted, and so a few believers withdrew to return to the potent expression of earlier days that had spread through the Greco-Roman world like wildfire. The original monks, now known as desert mothers and fathers, were ordinary people who wanted to continue living the common way of Jesus and the apostles. Those desert communities prayed like wild, unruly monks.

Acts is the biblical history book of the early church. I challenge you to read it in its entirety, highlighting every reference to "as we were going to the place of prayer" (or the equivalent phrase in your translation), and observe what comes along with a commitment to a life that is daily rooted in prayer.

In Acts 2, the flaming tongues of Pentecost descended while the believers were gathered *for morning prayer* (nine in the morning). In Acts 3, Peter and John performed the first miraculous healing after the resurrection *on the way to midday prayer* (three in the afternoon). In Acts 4, the foundations of the temple shook in response to the church's *ordinary prayer gathering*. In Acts 10, Peter received a vision that the gospel was for not just the Jewish people but the entire world, and the family of Jesus expanded to all nations *while praying midday prayers*.

Even in Acts 2, we read this summary of the church's inception: "They devoted themselves to the apostles' teaching and to fellowship, to the breaking of bread and to prayer."[19] The Greek word translated "prayer" is plural, a fact reflected in some translations, and almost certainly refers to the fixed rhythm of daily prayer.[20] And what followed that devotion to prayer? The early church's supernatural life included signs and wonders, wild generosity, countercultural community, and a daily tide of salvation washing in.[21]

The early Christians placed a higher value on gathering to pray than we commonly do today, and they possessed a higher concentration of the Spirit's power than we commonly do today. When we pray, expressing our love to God, the power of God, more or less, just inadvertently gets thrown in.

Throughout the whole of the biblical drama and into the early church history, prayer was the anchor of the Christian life in community. My suspicion is that when the apostle Paul instructed the church to "pray without ceasing,"[22] he had in mind both a constant state of interior being and an outward, committed, concrete rhythm. The invitation is something like "pray like a band of wild, unruly monks," and as you do, love and power will bloom together from within you.

Daily Prayer Rhythm

I'm not advocating a way of prayer that's novel, but one that's ancient. Like Isaac after the death of Abraham, I am redigging the wells the Philistines filled.[23] I am not digging a new well; rather, I'm just clearing the debris from the ancient forgotten wells, so that a new generation might come and drink.

The modern church is in desperate need of one of the church's most historic practices—one that has been largely forgotten in our time—a daily prayer rhythm. We can't merely look back and romanticize another time. The invitation is to live it now. Prayer, to return to where we began, is more practice than theory. If we want a biblical experience, we must live biblical lives, taking on biblical practices in a new time and place.

A daily prayer rhythm is about fidelity. It has absolutely everything to do with love and absolutely nothing to do with legalism. Jesus' personal discipline was always about freedom and life. When he rolled out of bed and made his way alone to the Mount of Olives to pray, it was love that drove him there, not a spiritual scorecard. For Jesus, being with the Father was his deepest desire, the source of identity, and only way to true life. "Discipline was, for Jesus, and should be for us, grounded in relationship and shaped by desire," writes psychologist David Benner.[24] God is not taking attendance or issuing grades. This is about love. To order your day according to intimacy with God is the lived intention to keep him as your first love.

Commitments, not feelings, are how we show our love. David Brooks defines a commitment as "falling in love with something [or someone] and then building a structure of behavior around it for those moments when love falters."[25] Jesus was getting at the same thing when he invited us to take on his "easy yoke."[26] And that's all a daily prayer rhythm is—a structure to support our deepest desires, even when our feelings and emotions betray us.

Jesus lived by a daily prayer rhythm in a world without iPhones or email, a world even without clocks. For Jesus and his earliest followers, communion with God marked the passage of time. Everything else happened a certain distance before or after prayer. Everything else was prioritized around prayer rather than prayer fitting in around competing priorities. Communion with the God of love was the center of life, the anchor for their every day.

What anchors your day right now? Possibly your workday demands, the buzz of notifications on your phone, or your email inbox? Your next meal or the number of passing hours till the weekend? The days marked off until your time of travel begins? Something sets the daily rhythm of your life. Something marks the passage of time. Whatever that something is, you owe it to yourself to think hard about these questions: *Is it making me whole? Does it love me or want to control me? Is it concerned for my deepest well-being or is it trying to sell me something? Is it shaping me into the best version of myself or is it frothing up my selfishness? Is it leaving me alive or is it leaving me exhausted?* Because whatever is at the center defines you and forms you into its image.

What if at the center of your every day, you placed communion with the God who personifies love? What if the waking thoughts of your day were spent dreaming with God—dreams as big as "kingdom come" and as ordinary as "daily bread"?[27] What if you slipped away at midday for a few minutes or a few seconds, because every other force is vying for your attention but only Jesus has your heart? What if you were to spend your commute home or the final moments before you fall asleep at night recounting the magnificent and minuscule ways you saw heaven pierce earth today? What if your day belonged to the God who loves you without needing to control you, the God whose chief concern is your deepest well-being, who is gently shaping you into the very best version of yourself and who breathes into your exhaustion with abundant life? What if fidelity to Jesus is everything, and the way you choose it is as simple as prayer?

This isn't a boisterous call to a more disciplined, legalistic, routine prayer life. It's a quiet rebellion, a free choice to live our lives by a different order of loves, marching to a different beat in the procession of another King.

Playing Jazz

The daily prayer rhythm observed in the early Christian centuries involved praying with the saints of biblical history. Sacred rhythms were honored for praying according to the Psalms, the Shema, which is made up of three biblical passages (Deuteronomy 6:4–9), and the Lord's Prayer.[28] The early Christians were formed and shaped in prayer by their ancient ancestors.

In recent generations, a resistance to disciplined, rhythmic prayer has emerged alongside the obsession with spontaneous, experiential prayer. Eugene Peterson observes:

> There is a prevailing bias among many American Christians against rote prayers, repeated prayers, "book" prayers—even when they are lifted directly from the "Jesus book." This is a

mistake. Spontaneities offer one kind of pleasure and taste of sanctity, repetitions another, equally pleasurable and holy. We don't have to choose between them. We *must not* choose between them. They are the polarities of prayer. The repetitions of our Lord's prayers (and David's) give us firm groundings for the spontaneities, the flights, the explorations, the meditations, the sighs, and the groans that go into the "prayer without ceasing" (1 Thess. 5:17 KJV) toward which Paul urges us.[29]

The modern church has forgotten the rhythm of prayer needed to nourish the spiritual life because we've bought into the illusion that spontaneous, memorably experiential prayer is the only authentic variety. But that view of authenticity is unrealistic and dysfunctional, not pure and discerning.

Prayer is like jazz. Jazz music is improvisational. Jazz bands don't stare at sheet music; they get lost in the music and let it carry them. A saxophonist in an orchestra sits with perfect posture in a refined, formal opera house. A saxophonist in a jazz trio plays with their back arched, their eyes closed, and an expression of deep satisfaction spread across their face inside a smoky, loud club. He is "feeling" the music, not reading it. The interesting thing about jazz, though, is that it requires a firm understanding of the instrument. A wealth of knowledge and hours of practice makes improvisation not only possible but enjoyable. In short, if you want to play jazz, you've got to learn the sheet music first. And if you want to pray with passion, spontaneity, and freedom, you've got to learn the sheet music.

On his knees in Gethsemane, sweating bloody drops of dread and anxiety, Jesus began to pray, "My Father, if it is not possible for this cup to be taken away unless I drink it, may your will be done."[30] It strikes me that Jesus' prayer in Matthew 26 is a mirror image of the Lord's Prayer in Matthew 6: "Our Father in heaven, hallowed be your name, your kingdom come, your will be done, on earth as it is in heaven."[31] The words that involuntarily spilled forth from his mouth in that moment of anguish bear a striking resemblance to the way he taught his disciples to pray years earlier. The circumstances couldn't have been more different, and yet the movements were identical. It has been said that, in times of chaos, we do not rise to the occasion; we fall to the level of our training. In the ultimate chaos, with the weight of the world's suffering on his shoulders, Jesus did not rise to the occasion; he fell to the level of his own training: "My Father . . . may your will be done."

Get these ancient, recited prayers into your bloodstream, and they'll come out of you when you need them most. The memorable moments of spontaneous prayer emerge from a rooted, disciplined life of prayer.

Herrnhut

Returning to the revival in Herrnhut, we see a real-life picture of rebellious fidelity to Jesus through prayer. The unlikely spark of the revival occurred when Count Nikolaus Ludwig von Zinzendorf welcomed those forty-eight refugees, chopping up the family property into the village of Herrnhut. They dreamed of recapturing the radical potency of the early church. A few years in, disillusioned, they came to the sober realization that their shared agreement and collective willpower weren't enough. Their vision was clean and inspiring off the eloquent lips of their leader but messy and ordinary in the context of relationship to one another.

Confronted by their own weakness, they finally started to pray like monks. Forty-eight refugees committed to a disciplined rhythm of daily prayer. Just five years into that commitment, a refugee village of thirty-two homes had inadvertently launched the greatest missions movement in world history.

The prayer meeting that started with those refugees went on, twenty-four hours a day, seven days a week, 365 days a year, for one hundred years—a century of unceasing prayer. The Moravian revival was a hundred-year prayer meeting that transformed the tiny village of Herrnhut into the missional base of the eighteenth century and the catalyst of the modern missions movement.

They weren't fanatics; they were radicals (from the Latin *radix*, "root").[32] They became radicals by growing deep roots through committed practice. They chose fidelity to Jesus, and he saves the best adventures for those who freely choose his love. They started praying like monks of the wildest and most undignified variety, and they ended up with a story even beyond their lofty vision. True radicals are always deeply rooted.

What was their secret? Plenty of people ask this question. Plenty of people want to bottle up and imitate the magic of the Moravian revival. In the words of Zinzendorf himself, here's the recipe: "I have one passion. It is He, only He."[33]

For them, it was all about love. The revival wasn't about a Savior with a missional strategy and a five-part plan; it was about a Savior who defends people when they're covered in shame, stands them up on their feet, looks them in the eye, and says, "Then neither do I condemn you."[34]

When that's your story, all that matters is remaining in that love. A daily prayer rhythm is not a fast track to revival or a hocus-pocus solution to drum up something powerful; it's a pathway to rebellious fidelity, to love expressed through prayer, to a commitment to keep on choosing him on all the ordinary days. The kingdom breaks in through those who seek it first, and that takes practice.

Rebellious fidelity—that's where the real treasures are.

PRACTICE

Daily Prayer Rhythm:
Morning, Midday, and Evening

Morning: The Lord's Prayer

Start your day with God. This simple practice is not about discipline or personality type; it's about love. I've yet to find any man or woman of faith whose impact for the kingdom of God left a significant mark who *didn't* spend the opening movements of the day in loving union with Jesus through prayer.

"Very early in the morning, while it was still dark, Jesus got up, left the house and went off to a solitary place, where he prayed."[35] As a thirteen-year-old, I read this verse, and it awoke the simplest of longings within me: *I want to pray like Jesus prayed.* So every night, I'd set my alarm clock fifteen minutes earlier than I had to (just fifteen minutes). I'd open my Bible to Mark 1 and lay it on top of my alarm clock. When the buzzer violently woke me up the following morning and my adolescent instinct to snooze took over, my right arm would swing over to the alarm clock and fall on top of these words: "Very early in the morning, while it was still dark, Jesus got up."

That simple habit presented me with a choice in the earliest movements of the day when my heart was willing but my flesh was weak. Beneath my surface-level desire for a few more minutes of sleep was a deeper desire to know the Father like Jesus did. And to borrow a phrase from John Mark Comer, "If you want to experience the life of Jesus, you have to adopt the lifestyle of Jesus."[36] That simple habit was the beginning of a life of prayer that became deeply personal, wildly adventurous, and wondrously awe-inducing.

Whatever your morning routine, I want to humbly suggest a new ambition, adjustment, or addition: pray like Jesus taught us.

Every morning, pray the Lord's Prayer. Jesus' instructive prayer found in Matthew 6 and Luke 11 is not only the literal application for how the Savior taught us to pray, but it's also the one documented way we are 100 percent sure the earliest church prayed liturgically.[37] When I suggest that you "pray the Lord's prayer," I don't mean recite the words as though it were a script. I mean allow those words to thematically move you through a very personal conversation with God.

Midday: The Lost

When speaking of people outside of a covenant relationship with God through salvation, Jesus often used the term *lost*. *Lost* describes a person searching for home, for safety, for rest, but lacking the certainty that they're headed in the right direction. It's a word of compassion, not categorization and certainly not condemnation. Jesus describes himself as the Good Shepherd in search of his lost sheep, even saying, "There will be more rejoicing in heaven over one sinner who repents than over ninety-nine righteous persons who do not need to repent."[38]

When we pray for the lost, several things are happening all at once. We are recovering the Shepherd's heart, allowing God to break our hearts for what breaks his own. We are taking up our authority as intercessors, calling heaven to act out of love for one another. And we are taking the risk of being sent, knowing that God often commissions us to go, incarnating our prayers with our hands and feet.

I want you to imagine this (indulge me for a moment). You—in the middle of your workday, whether that means sitting at a desk, driving a truck, running around a film set, calming a rowdy classroom, taking an order behind a cash register, or raising children—see yourself there at the midpoint of your day.

Now, you escape the flow of the workday for just a minute or two. It could be a moment of contemplative silence at your desk, a walk around the block outside your office building, or just an escape to a holy stall in the restroom. You're escaping because you know a secret. You know the secret that this kingdom that everyone is so feverishly building, willing their bodies and brains into a few more hours of productive focus, isn't the one that will stand. You know that there is a Father who draws souls to himself, a Good Shepherd in loving pursuit of his lost sheep. You steal away because you have to. You have to, or else you'll forget that secret. You'll start believing the same subtle lie that this small, temporary kingdom is the ultimate one, that your producing, not your loving, is of ultimate worth. You need to redirect your affections, your thoughts, the very center of your being, because it is by faithful, laboring prayer that God draws the lost to himself and reforms the passions of the praying person.

Evening: Gratitude

We tend to litter our dinner tables with the leftovers of the day. We carry the events of the day home with us, not because we want to, yet somehow we do. What if instead of spending your commute home stewing about an unpleasant interaction or planning how you'll handle a particular situation or wishing you had gotten one more thing done, you simply stood holding a subway pole or gripping your steering wheel and recounted everything you have to be grateful to God for from this day?

Morris West names a certain point in the spiritual journey when our prayer vocabulary gets summarized to only three phrases: "Thank you! Thank you! Thank you!"[39] To enjoy our lives, to savor our days, is sweet praise to God.

During the Jewish Passover, the Israelites traditionally sang a gratitude song called *dayenu*. *Dayenu* means "it would have been enough."[40] I once heard a pastor offer this translation: "Thank you, God, for overdoing it."

Dayenu prayers sound like, "God, lunch today would've been enough, but you provided me with the resources to choose the type of food I wanted to eat and options to pick from."

"God, lunch of my choice would've been enough, but you created a world of flavor and spice and culture to make food more than fuel—to offer it as artistic and delicious."

"God, a delicious lunch of my choice would've been enough, but you gave me a coworker to share a conversation with over that food."

"Thank you, God, for overdoing it."

That's *dayenu*. And in thirty seconds or thirty minutes, that's how we pray gratitude. This is such a small, manageable shift that will bear extraordinary fruit. What if you began to litter your dinner table with the fruit of the Spirit instead of the day's leftovers?

Daily Prayer Rhythm App

In partnership with 24-7 Prayer, I created the Inner Room app, which is a companion resource for the Daily Prayer Rhythm outlined in this practice. It includes both written and audio guides through morning, midday, and evening prayer. It is available in multiple languages, compatible with multiple devices, and can be downloaded wherever you get your apps. The Inner Room app can also be accessed at www. tylerstaton.com.

In addition, you can scan this QR code to watch a video and download the app.

RAISE UP THE TABERNACLE OF DAVID

In that day,

"I will restore David's fallen shelter—
I will repair its broken walls
and restore its ruins—
and will rebuild it as it used to be,
so that they may possess the remnant of Edom
and all the nations that bear my name,"
declares the Lord, *who will do these things.*
Amos 9:11–12

H ey, man, you want another seltzer?"
I looked up at him with tearstained cheeks.
"No man, I'm good."

It was just me and one other guy in the whole place, so the bartender was really motivated to keep the soda waters coming. He kept his distance after that brief interaction though. I get it.

Crying alone while hunched over a Bible isn't normal Irish pub behavior.

It was a Monday night in February. I was sitting alone at a pub reading—one of those pubs where everything is perpetually sticky and the only playlist is alt-rock from 1999. I was looking for a place to read at 9:30 p.m. on a Monday night and options were limited, so I walked in, took a seat at the bar, opened a Bible, and read these ancient words from the mostly forgotten prophet Amos:

In that day,

> "I will restore David's fallen shelter—
> I will repair its broken walls
> and restore its ruins—
> and will rebuild it as it used to be." (Amos 9:11)

So I'm sitting at the bar sipping a fizzy water, and as Matchbox Twenty plays over the unforgiving soundtrack, it's all crashing in on me—the story beneath Amos's prophecy.

The Story

So David went to bring up the ark of God from the house of Obed-Edom to the City of David with rejoicing. When those who were carrying the ark of the Lord had taken six steps, he sacrificed a bull and a fattened calf. Wearing a linen ephod, David was dancing before the Lord with all his might, while he and all Israel were bringing up the ark of the Lord with shouts and the sound of trumpets . . .

They brought the ark of the Lord and set it in its place inside the tent that David had pitched for it, and David sacrificed burnt offerings and fellowship offerings before the LORD. (2 Samuel 6:12–15, 17)

Seven years prior to the scene in 2 Samuel 6, David was anointed king of Israel. His path to the throne was unconventional, to say the least. Israel's first king, Saul, was so threatened by David that he spent a good chunk of his time hunting him from town to town, trying to kill him—a real-life *Most Dangerous Game*. Finally, after Saul's death, David was anointed king. But then Ish-Bosheth, one of Saul's sons, moved into the palace uninvited, surrounded it with a militia, and took the throne by force. So David has been living in a small town in the countryside, waiting for this imposter to stop sleeping in his royal bed—for *seven years*. That's plenty of time to daydream about a royal entrance into the city. It's plenty of time to come up with a political strategy.

That's what makes David's entrance so shocking. This is his long-awaited royal parade, his coronation day, his triumphal entry. And it was jaw-dropping.

No doubt people heard him coming before they saw the parade. An entire army was marching and singing a song David himself composed for the occasion. The lyrics are in our Bible, and we call it Psalm 24:

> Lift up your heads, you gates;
>> be lifted up, you ancient doors,
>> that the King of glory may come in.[1]

That sounds about right for a royal parade, doesn't it?

> Who is this King of glory?
>> The LORD strong and mighty,
>> the LORD mighty in battle.[2]

Wait, what? David *isn't* the king of glory? Is that a typo? David is an experienced songwriter. He knows what he's doing. And this is the chorus, so it's repeated in the psalm:

> Lift up your heads, you gates;
>> lift them up, you ancient doors,
>> that the King of glory may come in.
> Who is he, this King of glory?
>> The Lord Almighty—
>> he is the King of glory.[3]

King David enters to a song of praise, but he's not the king the song is praising. "The Lord Almighty—he is the King of glory."

About that time, the march crested the hill and started coming down into Jerusalem. The onlooking crowd expected to see a long march of soldiers and magicians, the king carried on the ancient equivalent of a parade float, sitting on his throne, decorated in royal robes and wearing a heavy crown on his head. That's how Saul likely came in. That's what they were waiting to see.

What they actually saw was David, their new king, at the front of the parade, wearing a linen ephod, and he's dancing. A linen ephod—that's the outfit David chose for his big day, not the expected royal robe and a crown. An ephod was a priestly garment, not an aristocratic one. It wasn't the dignified outer robe either; it was the undergarment of a priest. David was symbolically saying, "I'm not a king who is coming to sit on a throne; I'm a priest coming to lead you into the presence of God. But I'm the least of all the priests, unqualified to wear the robes and the tassels."

Here comes the new king. David is singing a song of praise to God, and he's dancing in a priest's underwear. It's foolish, but it's a holy kind of foolishness.

There's a float at the back of the parade, but instead of housing a throne for David to sit on, it holds the ark of the covenant. The ark was a sacred wooden box carried by the Israelites through the desert during the exodus, symbolizing God's presence with them. This box was the intersection between heaven and earth. When God's people took the promised land, the ark led the procession through the parted waters of the Jordan River.

When things got comfortable, King Saul left the ark in a foreign field. That's what tends to happen with God. We leave him behind when we get comfortable. David hunted down the ark and placed it on the throne. God, the true King, on the seat of honor. David, the dancing priest, celebrating God's return to his people.

Every jaw is on the ground while David makes his way down Broadway. When he gets to the town square, he has arranged for a tent at the city center, right outside the palace doors—a tent in the form of Moses's tent of meeting, where Israel's great deliverer spoke face-to-face with God as one speaks to a friend. David puts the ark back in the tent and calls it a "tabernacle."[4]

Don't picture a dazzling, ornate temple. We're not even talking about something alternative and edgy. The English word *tabernacle* translates the Hebrew *sukkah*, which means "booth" or "shelter." It was an unimpressive, makeshift, temporary shelter, something like what we'd call a tent today. David's big idea, the culmination of seven years of waiting and dreaming, was, "What if we pitched a tent? A tent where anyone and everyone can come to worship and pray. Nothing fancy, just a common space right at the city center for prayer."

When a new president is elected, they have a first order of business to tackle immediately—something promised to voters, a pet project chosen to define their legacy. David's very first act on his very first day as Israel's king was to reconstruct Moses's tent of meeting in the city center. At first, his royal advisers may have thought the tent was just a symbol, a way to remember the exodus.

"Sure," they must have thought, "I'm all for celebrating history." But for David, this tent was more than a symbol; it was a statement of value and a threat to the status quo.

After his entrance, David went into the palace, sat down with his board of advisers, and laid out the plan. David hired 288 worship leaders, prophets, and elders to pray and worship in that tent, presumably twenty-four hours a day.[5] He was a king leading a military during an era of tribal warfare, and he just emptied the national savings account for prayer. Can you imagine the meeting where he laid out that strategic plan? "Uhhh, Dave, we're gonna need to beef up our defenses against the armies that are literally surrounding us, and you want to spend it all on a prayer tent?"

"Yeah. That's exactly right."

Then he did it.

For the thirty-three years of David's reign as Israel's king, worship and prayer took place twenty-four hours a day. David put prayer back at the very center of God's people. And he invited everyone—men and women, slave and free, Israelite and pagan. The thirty-three years of David's kingship were the only time before the resurrection that there were no restrictions on access to God's presence. David's tabernacle was a New Testament reality in an Old Testament world. That's the scandal of this prayer tent.

I have this dream for the church: prayer at the center of God's people. I dream about a freestanding space right in the heart of my city where anyone and everyone can come to pray. A space consecrated by the prayers of so many who have saturated it in praise, hope, and longing. A space that inadvertently gives birth to a wave of mission that looks something like the kingdom of God set loose on a city. That's what I dream of for the church.

But the modern church's best-kept secret is this: we believe in productivity, not prayer. We believe in solid programs, above-average teaching, and yet another worship album release. That's success right? The church's underground atheism in our time is that we will busy ourselves with almost anything except prayer.

David's jaw-dropping first move was to put prayer back at the center for God's people. That was either the most admirable or the most ridiculous move a king could make, depending on if you lean more poet or pragmatist, but David's unconventional reign as king was the political high point of Israelite history any way you measure it—peace and safety in the city, prosperity in the economy, care for the poor, a divided kingdom unified. David's priorities looked like a political disaster on paper, but he built his life radically on prayer, and God took care of everything else. As David Fritch writes, "The presence of God was David's political strategy."[6]

The pattern that emerges from David's tabernacle is this: prioritize presence in the church, and you get the kingdom in the city.

Houses of Prayer

"Hey, man, you want another seltzer?"

There I was, with tears in my eyes in that Irish pub. I'm being serenaded by Rob Thomas, and I'm dreaming of David's prayer tent. I left and wandered the streets, praying the prayer of Amos: "O Lord, raise up David's tabernacle here. In our days. In our city. Raise up the tabernacle of David."[7]

From that night on, I started spending every Monday night walking the streets of Brooklyn praying the prayer of Amos: "O Lord, do that in our days. Do that here. Do that through us. Raise up David's tabernacle in my time and place."

The glory of Amos's prophecy is that the early church brought it off the page and into the world. It came alive in secret meetings held in underground Roman basements. Communities were formed that put prayer at the center for God's people, and the kingdom spilled into the city in such a profound way that the world has never recovered.

The tragedy of Amos's prophecy is that after David, the next generation of political advisers went back to board meetings and military strategy. And after Jesus reenacted David's dramatic entrance in his own triumphal entry, the very priests who witnessed it all, the ones who could recite the facts of David's tabernacle from memory—they weren't in those Roman basements. They picked up the coins and put them back in the cash registers, returned every dove to its cage, tidied up the mess.

I have a dream for the church. We will become houses of prayer again. None of us want to spend the rest of our lives cloistered off in socially irrelevant, spiritually dry weekly meetings. What's the alternative? The radical reprioritization of prayer. And if the cost is foolishness, count me in. If the cost is sacrifice, count me in. If the cost is faith, count me in. If the cost is perseverance, count me in.

A yes to this kind of kingdom vision looks less like gritting our teeth and more like a king dancing in a priest's underwear. It looks less like putting our nose to the grindstone and more like Jesus smiling ear to ear on the back of a donkey half his weight. It looks less like intensity, and a lot more like joy.

ACKNOWLEDGMENTS

This book was penned by my hand, but the words of this book were first written on my heart by so many.

Kirsten, thank you for loving me enough to put up with my stubborn and absurd insistence on ordering my life around communion with Jesus through prayer. Hank, Simon, and Amos, I pray that my ceiling in prayer will be your floor.

Thank you to the 24-7 Prayer Movement, and to Pete Greig in particular, for putting into language the longings of my heart and welcoming me into the fold.

The cluttered early drafts of this book were made coherent by the patient editing of Gemma Ryan, Simon Morris, Will Thomas, John Mark Comer, Jared Boyd, Tim Mackie, Peter Quint, Morgan Davis, Bethany Allen, Gerald Griffin, Gavin Bennett, Brett Leyde, and Gerry Breshears.

Thank you to Oaks Church Brooklyn and Bridgetown Church for both hearing and enfleshing this book's contents before it was written.

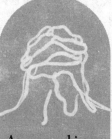

THE INTERCESSION
OF CHRIST

*Therefore he is able to save completely those who
come to God through him, because he always
lives to intercede for them.*

Hebrews 7:25

Jesus' birth was accompanied by an angelic soundtrack: "Glory to God in the highest heaven, and on earth peace to those on whom his favor rests."[1] That's a lot more than a Christmas carol. It's a political statement, inspired by the prophet Isaiah who added, "For to us a child is born, to us a son is given, and the government will be on his shoulders."[2] Sure, he's a child meek and mild today. But make no mistake about it. This child is here to reign. Heaven and earth agree on that.

For thirty years, it looked a lot like he couldn't live up to the hype. Then, following a dove-doting baptism and an apparently paradigm-shifting forty-day pilgrimage into the desert, he showed back up, talking a big game. Jesus strolled right into the synagogue, read Isaiah's words of the promised messianic ministry, and closed the sermon with, "Today this scripture is fulfilled in your hearing."[3]

The next thirty-six months were astonishing. He was unstoppable. He made outcasts into heroes. He won every argument against the establishment. He turned funerals into celebrations, kept wedding receptions alive till sunrise, and turned street corners into synagogues. He granted forgiveness without a confessional booth, healed without a medical license, and taught a master class without a formal education.

His arrival in a rural village made the Beatles in their prime look like a local band trying to make it big. When he came to Jerusalem, the crowds ripped branches off the trees and pulled the shirts off their own backs just so his colt wouldn't have to lay a hoof on the dirt road. "Hosanna! Blessed is he who comes in the name of the Lord! Blessed is the coming kingdom of our father David! Hosanna in the highest heaven!"[4] Another political statement, this one even more emphatic. *Hosanna* is an ancient Jewish declaration that means, "Save!" And they used that word as the chorus and filled in the verses with the words of Psalm 118. In other words, "Here is the one. The one who's come to reign. The one who's come to save. Here is God in the flesh, arriving to sit on his throne once and for all." What Jesus claimed in the synagogue three years earlier had come to pass.

That's what made his public execution a week later so disorienting. But he even managed to turn crucifixion into a victory cry more inspiring than William Wallace in blue face paint on horseback: "It is finished!"[5] A victorious crucifixion? Who has ever heard of such a thing? And yet Jesus' actions showed that when the Roman soldiers planted a cross in the ground with his gangly body spread out on it, it was the equivalent of a king planting a flag in enemy-occupied territory to claim land for himself. God takes creation back. *It is finished!*

Only, nothing seemed finished. In fact, nothing seemed to change at all in the days and weeks following that victory cry. Herod still occupied the throne, ruling like a corrupt autocrat. Every street was still patrolled by Roman soldiers who were oppressing 99 percent of the indigenous population. The temple curtain that had been torn down the middle was sewn back up, and the priests kept on restricting access to God for some. The streets outside still overflowed with poor beggars without a roof to find shelter under and suffering patients without a doctor to receive treatment from.

The same day Jesus healed a blind man, ten more were born blind who didn't receive sight. The night he invited a prostitute to be honored company at his dinner table, a hundred others were objectified by another sleazy patron. The day he rehabilitated one tax collector, plenty of others exploited the poor out of their last penny. And the day after he died looked a whole lot like the day before.

Even his own disciples didn't seem to buy the victory initially, unless your idea of a victory march looks like hiding out in an upper room biting your fingernails, afraid to be seen and identified as a co-conspirator.

Where is the kingdom that outlasts all the others? The one the gates of hell can't prevail against? The overthrow of the oppressor all those people with palm fronds were crying out for?

It Doesn't *Feel* Finished

The Christian belief is that Jesus' death satisfied the wages of sin. His resurrection defeated death, not only for him, but for all who call him Lord. The life, death, and resurrection of Jesus was a complete thirty-three-year work that cut a hole in the heavy, suffocating blanket that fell on humanity in response to sin. It is finished, and it's available to anyone and everyone by grace.

That's a beautiful idea. The trouble is that it tends to stay in the realm of ideas. We can't seem to drive the story of Jesus from our head into our hearts. We sing about it, read about it, listen to it told and retold through a thousand metaphors. We ingest it in bread and wine, the sensation of grace running through our taste buds. But we just can't seem to make this story come alive in our bones. We can't seem to live like we're free and enjoy today like it doesn't hold the weight of the world.

There remains that nagging part of our lives we withhold from grace, assuming we still have some active role to play. We're convinced we have to overcome, to change, to mature, to become. We turn grace into a diet plan and Jesus into a calorie counter. He's here to whip us into shape, but make no mistake, we still have to put in the work to achieve the desired results. The heart longs for grace, but the mind resists it. We are, it seems, too weak to simply receive.

There was something else Jesus said on the cross. Words I imagine he whispered feebly, voice quivering, before he got to that upside-down victory cry: "My God, my God, why have you forsaken me?"[6]

That's a prayer I can get behind, one I can identify with. "Where are you, God?" I've whispered that prayer under my breath, my own voice quivering, more times than I can count. These words weren't original to Jesus. He's borrowing from the Psalms, the original hymnal, to pray the words of David that open Psalm 22. Scripture is careful to note, though, that Jesus didn't pray it in the polished, refined Hebrew it was first written in. Jesus prayed it in Aramaic, the common language of the pubs and schoolyards: "*Eli, Eli, lema sabachthani?*" According to New Testament scholar Richard Bauckham, by praying this in the Aramaic, Jesus was personalizing the psalm.[7] He wasn't just noting that he seemed to be experiencing something of what David had described all those years before; he was crying across history—past, present, and future—his voice echoing from beginning to end, "Where are you, God?" What David prayed in Psalm 22, what I've prayed so many times before and am bound to pray again, was concentrated and fulfilled in Jesus.

The redemption accomplished by Jesus, no matter how long and fervently I believe it, no matter how eloquently it's remembered and reimagined, just never seems to *feel* finished. And that admission is the precise point where intercession, the present work of Jesus Christ, begins.

Our praying lives are incomplete without an understanding of the present praying life of Christ because prayer doesn't begin with us; it begins with Jesus. His prayers always precede our prayers.

The Intercession of Christ

Interceding. That's what Jesus is doing right now, between his first and second coming.

It's a strange word in both ancient and modern language. We don't use it in common conversation today, and the ancient Greeks didn't either. Biblically, you'll find it only a few times in the New Testament.[8] The English word *intercede* translates the Greek *entynchano*, which means "plead, appeal for, petition." So, who is Jesus pleading to, appealing for, petitioning? God the Father. On your behalf. And mine.

Jesus is praying for you and me. He is the bridge between the Father's heavenly resources and our earthly lives. Let me be clear. The Father does not require more convincing to embrace us as his own, and the Son doesn't care for us more deeply than the Father does. This is reflective of the triune mystery of a three-in-one, communal God. It is the Son's great passion to see his atoning work become our current experience and the Father's deep joy to say an unhesitating yes to the Son's intercession.

Christ's heavenly intercession affirms the sufficiency of his earthly life. The atonement was the finished work of accomplishing our salvation. Intercession is the present work of applying our salvation. Put in layperson's terms, Jesus finished the work of redemption on the cross, but his heavenly prayers for you and me apply the experience of that victory to the present moment.

The New Testament unmistakably joins the two together. "Who will bring any charge against those whom God has chosen? It is God who justifies. Who then is the one who condemns? No one. Christ Jesus who died—more than that, who was raised to life—is at the right hand of God and is also interceding for us."[9]

Romans 5 speaks of justification in the past tense: "Therefore, since we *have been* justified through faith, we have peace with God."[10] It's a done deal. A past work. Finished.

Colossians 3 speaks of glorification as the sure future: "When Christ, who is your life, appears, *then* you also will appear with him in glory."[11] The end of the story is written. We are justified by what he's done (past work) and glorified by what he will do (future work).

Hebrews 7 speaks of intercession in the present: "he *always lives* to intercede for them."[12]

Intercession is the present action of Jesus that pulls at this story from both ends—the salvation work accomplished in the past and the glory that awaits us in the future. Intercession, stated as simply as possible, brings forth the image of Jesus praying for us, individually by name. And as he does, he wedges us tightly between forgiveness and glory, enabling a deep inner rest sheltered by security, hope, and delight.

Sibling Rivalry

I am the middle child of three boys—one eighteen months older, and one fifteen months younger. Sibling rivalry was a given in my family. My older brother, Josh, and I were both really into sports, and he was better—way better. But by the time I was about twelve, the tables were turning when it came to baseball. He was still bigger, stronger, faster, but I had him in baseball. If little brother is catching you for the first time—in anything—that's a moment provoking insecurity.

One of the traditions in baseball is that the home team hangs up *K*s on the scoreboard for every strikeout the pitcher gets.[13] *K* stands for "strikeout" in a baseball scorebook, and the tradition really took off among beer-chugging fans in the left field bleachers.

When I was twelve, I was the pitcher on my Little League team. Josh came to every one of my games and hung *K*s on the fence for every strikeout. He'd get there early, bum a stack of napkins from the concession stand, and pull out the Sharpie he had brought from home to document every strikeout. He'd make *K*s so bold they bled through a stack of five napkins, and then he'd wrap the corners around the gray wire fence, screaming like a diehard fan in a three-row bleacher full of half-interested parents.

That's the opposite of the sibling rivalry we're all so familiar with. And that's what comes to mind when I think of Christ's heavenly intercession—my big brother in the bleachers at my Little League game. It's one thing to be told your brother supports you; it's another thing to *experience* that support in the form of full-throated screams and Sharpie-saturated napkins like you're pitching in game seven of the World Series. Justification is the knowledge of Christ's heart; intercession is the application of that very heart. It's the experience.

Intercession takes biblical rumors and makes them real within us. Scripture teaches that God is a loving Father who is interested in the mundane, day-to-day of my existence, but Christ's intercession makes that real to me. Scripture says that God is love, that the deep longing of his heart is simply to be with me forever, but Christ's intercession makes that real to me. Scripture claims that God is ever running out to meet me, clothing me in royal robes, and welcoming me to the home I wandered away from before I really even knew what I was leaving, but it's Jesus' intercession that makes that real to me.

Intercession means Jesus is not cool and reserved. He's passionate, interested, invested, engaged. Even now, as your eyes scan over these words, Jesus is applying the finished work of the cross to you. He's lavishing you in the Father's love, assuring you of your forgiveness, binding up your wounds, and breathing courage into your lungs. Intercession means all that.

In spite of the magnificent truth of justification, everyone I've ever met, regardless of the strength of their belief, has some pocket of their lives where they insist on covering for themselves, giving away their disbelief that the forgiveness of Jesus is sufficient to cover this—to cover this again, to cover this no matter how many times it takes.

Dane Ortlund writes:

God's forgiving, redeeming, restoring touch reaches down into the darkest crevices of our souls, those places where we are most ashamed, most defeated. More than this: those crevices of sin are themselves the places where Christ loves us the most. His heart willingly goes there. His heart is *most* strongly drawn there. He knows us to the uttermost, and he saves us to the uttermost, because his heart is drawn out to us to the uttermost. We cannot sin our way out of his tender care . . . Our sinning goes to the uttermost. But his saving goes to the uttermost. And his saving always outpaces and overwhelms our sinning, because he always lives to intercede for us.[14]

Hebrews 7:25 reads, "[Jesus] is able to save completely." The English word *completely* translates the Greek *panteles*, a word summarizing the idea of "comprehensiveness, completeness, exhaustive wholeness."[15] You'll only find it one other place in the Bible—Luke 13:11, when Jesus healed a woman who had been disabled for eighteen years. Luke writes that the woman was bent over, unable to straighten up *panteles* ("at all"). The point made in Hebrews is that Jesus doesn't just make a way for you and me to hobble through life and make it to the end in one piece; he makes a way for us to stand up straight, run, jump, dance, and laugh in the face of death! That—the today experience of the cosmic reality won for us in his life—is his heavenly intercession, the prayer of Jesus.

Yada

In his book *Abba's Child*, Brennan Manning wrote about a twenty-day silent retreat he took to a cabin in Colorado. Nothing to distract himself with, nothing to look forward to—just alone and present for twenty days.

Manning met God as an alcoholic at the end of his rope and journeyed his way out of crippling addiction through prayer. But that was a long time ago. At the time of this retreat, he was eighteen years into a newfound calling as a Franciscan priest. He was a sought-after speaker and a renowned author.

In the activity of public life, Manning was an accomplished spiritual guide. Alone and undistracted, though, he was confronted by the gap between spiritual theory and actual experience: "The great divorce between my head and my heart had endured throughout my ministry. For eighteen years I proclaimed the good news of God's passionate, unconditional love—utterly convicted in my head but not feeling it in my heart. I never felt loved."[16] He carried a false view of himself first into alcoholism and second into religion. He had been both the younger and the older brother in the prodigal son parable, and now, alone on a mountain hike with no one to become and no one to impress, he was invited by God to shed the false self and be loved.

Manning always believed in the love of God. He studied it, illustrated it, wrote about it, spoke about it, counseled people toward it. But stripped of all distraction, activity, and busyness, on a mountain with nothing to dress himself up with—that's where he *knew* the love of God.

In the English language, we typically understand "belief" to be deeper and more personal than "knowledge." Knowledge is purely intellectual; belief is gut-level conviction. Knowledge is the language of the head; belief is the language of the heart. But that's not the Hebrew understanding of knowledge.

The Hebrew word for knowledge is *yada*, and it's a relational knowing. If you were to ask me, "How do you know that your wife loves you?" I'd begin to tell you about the way our relationship works. I'd describe all the little ways she chooses my company, all the times she's stuck with me when I was wrong or lost or difficult, all the occasions she's been a rock of support, and all the fun evenings of laughter, meals shared, and memories of doing nothing together. What is all that? It's relational knowledge. I've experienced her love. That's how I know.

The Hebrew *yada* is even used in the Old Testament as a euphemism for sex. "Now Adam knew Eve his wife, and she conceived."[17] That sort of thing. That's because knowledge, in the Hebrew understanding, was intimate. It was not memorized in a classroom but experienced in a relationship. Spiritual knowledge has to be inhabited, experienced, lived.

Novelist and pastor Frederick Buechner summarizes: "For what we need to know, of course, is not just that God exists, not just that beyond the steely brightness of the stars there is a cosmic intelligence of some kind that keeps the whole show going, but that there is a God right here in the thick of our day-by-day lives . . . It is not objective proof of God's existence that we want but the experience of God's presence. That is the miracle that we are really after, and that is also, I think, the miracle that we really get."[18]

It's not enough to believe in the accepting love of God. We have to allow God to love us exactly as we are, naked and unashamed.[19] By Christ's intercession, the love of God seeps into every crack of our inner world, and the Spirit opens our eyes to discover ourselves as we really are—fixed in the gaze of God's love.

The Face of Christ

I had hardly slept, but I was wide awake. My eyes darted around the room for a moment or two as I remembered where I was. I had flown across the United States the night before, rented a car, and driven to the abbey, the chosen destination for a prayer retreat with two close friends. I barely made it without falling asleep at the wheel, but I made it. It was 6:00 a.m. I had slept just five hours, and my body hadn't caught up to a new time zone.

I splashed water in my face at the bathroom sink and walked out of my room to get a cup of coffee as the first rays of sun silhouetted the evergreen trees covering the hills in the distance. I'm used to being awake before anyone else. I love the morning. I love the shock to my lungs with the first breath of crisp, cool air; the taste of that first sip of hot coffee; and the first word of prayer uttered each new day. But today I was far from alone. In fact, I might've been the last one up.

I was surrounded by monks, old and young. There were monks who must've been older than ninety, and others who couldn't have been a day past twenty-five—all of whom had committed to an ancient, simple way of life. They were preserving a way of community, hospitality, and prayer mostly forgotten in the blur of the modern world. And they weren't preserving it in books on library shelves, but in their enfleshed lives.

Eastern Orthodox Bishop Kallistos Ware writes, "Christianity is not merely a philosophical theory or a moral code, but involves a direct sharing in divine life and glory, a transforming union with God 'face to face.'"[20]

Monks of various traditions are instructed to picture the face of Jesus as they pray. It's an anchor, a point where their prayers always must return. We come with our requests, but it's him we are really seeking. We want to see him face-to-face. And in the face of Christ, we discover the hospitality of God. The greatest scandal of all is that Jesus brought prayer too close, made God too accessible. Prayer does not emerge from knowing our needs but from knowing God's heart.

It Is Finished

As noted earlier, the heartbreaking prayer of Jesus from the cross— "My God, my God, why have you forsaken me?"—was the first line of Psalm 22. Jesus recited a Davidic psalm in front of a majority Jewish crowd. Everyone in the crowd would've recited this prayer from childhood. They knew it by heart. Jesus prayed the first line, and that was all he needed to do. Every face in the crowd knew where it ended. Psalm 22 opened with the expression of debilitating isolation and emotional turmoil. That's where it started, but that wasn't where it ended.

> For he has not despised or scorned
>> the suffering of the afflicted one;
> he has not hidden his face from him
>> but has listened to his cry for help.
>
> From you comes the theme of my praise in the great
>> assembly;
>> before those who fear you I will fulfill my vows.
>> (Psalm 22:24–25)

It ended not in despair but in exultation, not in isolation but community. When Jesus prayed Psalm 22 from the cross, he was praying in place of all of us. He was interceding.

The reality of his atoning work is constant, but the experience of that very work comes in fits and starts, breakthroughs and droughts, moments of divine assurance followed by bouts of human insecurity. And because of that, Jesus is praying for you right now.

One of my most frequent prayers is to simply try to get in touch with his prayers for me. I usually phrase it as a question: "Jesus if you were to walk in the room right now, what would you want to say to me?" Ask him. Be still and wait. In my experience, he's eager to share his heart.

Appendix 2

A GRID FOR SEARCHING AND NAMING

The ancients practiced confession within four categories. These may be helpful to keep in mind as a grid for searching your own inner life, with the Spirit as your guide.

1. **Blatant.** These are sins universally recognized in both secular culture and the kingdom of God. Obvious examples are murder or any other form of violence against an innocent person, acting on lust in a way that endangers or discomforts another, expressions of anger summed up under the heading of "rage," greed for material gain that actively oppresses a victimized party, and the like.

2. **Deliberate.** These are sins (usually outward, behavioral sins) recognized in the kingdom of God but not in the broader, secular culture. For example, think of food sacrificed to idols in the early church era and the bounds of healthy sexual expression in the modern church era.

3. **Unconscious.** Unconscious sins are deeper thought patterns that give birth or lead to expressed sin. These sin patterns usually live far enough beneath the surface

that they are unseen without intentional space for self-examination. Examples include, but are not limited to, the tendency to prioritize productivity over people; to define oneself by success, accomplishment, or reputation; or to live in a state of relational codependency with an individual or group.

4. **Inner Orientations.** Sin, at its deepest and most hidden, is about disordered trust structures. Ask yourself this question: *Who am I really trusting?* Behavior effortlessly (and often destructively) flows from there. Traditionally, these trust structures are called the "false self." When we begin to notice our self-made trust structures for drumming up our own significance, sense of well-being, and security, we begin to notice the particular "fig leaves" we've picked out to cover up with.

NOTES

Foreword

1. Thomas Keating, *Open Mind, Open Heart: The Contemplative Dimension of the Gospel* (New York: Continuum, 1992), 137, italics in original.

Introduction

1. See George H. Gallup Jr., *Religion in America 1996* (Princeton, NJ: Princeton Religion Research Center, 1996), 4, 12, 19.
2. See Leonardo Blair, "Fewer Than Half of American Adults Pray Daily; Religiously Unaffiliated Grows: Study," *Christian Post*, December 17, 2021, www.christianpost.com/news/fewer-than-half-of-american -adults-pray-daily-study.html.
3. Abraham Joshua Heschel, *Man's Quest for God: Studies in Prayer and Symbolism* (New York: Scribner, 1954), 5, italics in original.
4. See Deuteronomy 4:29; Proverbs 8:17; Jeremiah 29:13; Matthew 7:7; Luke 11:9; Acts 17:24–28.

Chapter 1: Holy Ground

1. Exodus 3:5.
2. John 15:7.
3. Philippians 4:5–7.
4. See "Mobile Fact Sheet," Pew Research Center, April 7, 2021, www .pewresearch.org/internet/fact-sheet/mobile.
5. Dallas Willard, *The Spirit of the Disciplines: Understanding How God Changes Lives* (San Francisco: HarperSanFrancisco, 1988), 163.
6. See Matthew 7:16–20.
7. See Hebrews 11:1.

8. David did not write all the psalms; however, he wrote about half of them, and he is the author of the psalms selected in this example.

9. Psalm 140:10.

10. Psalm 69:3.

11. Psalm 142:2.

12. See Matthew 5:43–44; Exodus 34:6.

13. See 1 Samuel 13:14; Acts 13:22.

14. C. S. Lewis, *Letters to Malcolm, Chiefly on Prayer* (New York: Harcourt, Brace & World, 1964), 22.

15. Matthew 6:11.

16. Roberta C. Bondi, *To Pray and to Love: Conversations on Prayer with the Early Church* (Minneapolis: Fortress, 1991), 49.

17. John 2:16.

18. Nancy Mairs, *Ordinary Time: Cycles in Marriage, Faith, and Renewal* (Boston: Beacon, 1993), 54.

19. Pete Greig, *Dirty Glory: Go Where Your Best Prayers Take You* (Colorado Springs: NavPress, 2016), 53.

20. "Earth's Moon: Quick Facts," NASA Science, https://moon.nasa.gov /about/in-depth.

21. Luke 11:1.

22. Richard Foster, *Prayer: Finding the Heart's True Home* (New York: HarperCollins, 1992), 13.

23. Quoted in Br. David Steindl-Rast, "Man of Prayer," in *Thomas Merton/Monk: A Monastic Tribute*, ed. Patrick Hart (New York: Sheed & Ward, 1974), 79.

24. Mother Teresa, *No Greater Love*, eds. Becky Benenate and Joseph Durepos (Novato, CA: New World Library, 1997), 6.

25. Dom John Chapman, *The Spiritual Letters of Dom John Chapman* (London: Sheed & Ward, 1935), 25.

26. See Luke 23:32–43.

27. Ted Loder, "There Is Something I Wanted to Tell You," in *Guerrillas of Grace: Prayers for the Battle*, 20th anniversary edition (Minneapolis: Augsburg Fortress, 2004), 67–68. Used by permission.

Chapter 2: Be Still and Know

1. Philip Yancey, *Prayer: Does It Make Any Difference?* (Grand Rapids: Zondervan, 2006), 29.

2. Psalm 46:10.

3. All the heavy lifting for the research that follows was done by my friend John Mark Comer. The ideas in this section were borrowed with his generous permission. For a fuller treatment of this topic, there is no better source than his book *The Ruthless Elimination of Hurry* (Colorado Springs: WaterBrook, 2019).

4. See Carl Honoré, *In Praise of Slowness: Challenging the Cult of Speed* (San Francisco: HarperSanFrancisco, 2004).

5. Cited in Dr. James B. Maas, *Power Sleep: The Revolutionary Program That Prepares Your Mind for Peak Performance* (1998; repr., New York: Quill, 2001), 7.

6. See Kerby Anderson, *Technology and Social Trends: A Biblical Point of View* (Cambridge, OH: Christian Publishing House, 2016), 102.

7. Sarah O'Connor, "Commentary: The Mysterious Recent Decline of Our Leisure Time," CNA, October 7, 2021, www.channelnewsasia .com/commentary/leisure-time-decline-less-why-do-i-feel-busy -work-home-2225276, emphasis added.

8. Cited in Julia Naftulin, "Here's How Many Times We Touch Our Phones Every Day," *Business Insider*, July 13, 2016, www.business insider.com/dscout-research-people-touch-cell-phones-2617-times-a -day-2016-7.

9. See Eileen Brown, "Americans Spend Far More Time on Their Smartphones Than They Think," ZDNet, April 28, 2019, www .zdnet.com/article/americans-spend-far-more-time-on-their-smart phones-than-they-think.

10. Dallas Willard, *Living in Christ's Presence: Final Words on Heaven and the Kingdom of God* (Downers Grove, IL: InterVarsity, 2013), 144.

11. Michael Zigarelli, "Distracted from God: A Five-Year, Worldwide Study," Christianity 9 to 5, 2008, www.christianity9to5.org /distracted-from-god.

12. Quoted in Morton T. Kelsey, *The Other Side of Silence: A Guide to Christian Meditation* (New York: Paulist, 1976), 83.

13. Richard Foster, *Celebration of Discipline: The Path to Spiritual Growth* (San Francisco: Harper & Row, 1978), 13.

14. Cited in Yancey, *Prayer*, 24.

15. Thomas Kelly, *A Testament of Devotion* (1941; repr., New York: Walker, 1987), 156.

16. Kelly, *Testament of Devotion*, 158.

17. See Genesis 3.

18. Ronald Rolheiser, *Sacred Fire: A Vision for a Deeper Human and Christian Maturity* (New York: Image, 2014), 200.

19. See Jason Dorrier, "How Many Galaxies Are in the Universe? A New Answer from the Darkest Sky Ever Observed," SingularityHub, January 15, 2021, https://singularityhub.com/2021/01/15/how -many-galaxies-are-in-the-universe-a-new-answer-emerges-from -the-darkest-sky-ever-observed.

20. See "Milky Way," Western Washington University Physics/ Astronomy Dept., www.wwu.edu/astro101/a101_milkyway.shtml.

21. See Marina Koren, "When Will Voyager Stop Calling Home?," *Atlantic*, September 5, 2017, www.theatlantic.com/science/archive /2017/09/voyager-interstellar-space/538881.

22. See Passant Rabie, "After Months of Silence, Voyager 2 Sends a Gleeful Message Back to Earth," Inverse, November 3, 2020, www .inverse.com/science/voyager-2-finally-phones-home.

23. See Stacey Leasca, "Here's What Actually Happens When You Travel at the Speed of Light, According to NASA," *Travel + Leisure*, August 26, 2020, www.travelandleisure.com/trip-ideas/space-astronomy /nasa-near-light-speed-travel.

24. Psalm 146:3–4 ESV.

25. Psalm 39:4–5.

26. Genesis 3:4.

27. Henri Nouwen, *The Way of the Heart: Desert Spirituality and Contemporary Ministry* (San Francisco: Harper & Row, 1981), 25–26.

28. See Psalms 56:8; 139:17–18.

29. Hans Urs von Balthasar, *Prayer*, trans. Graham Harrison (San Francisco: Ignatius, 1986), 44.

30. Psalm 46:10.

31. Psalm 42:7.

Chapter 3: Our Father

1. For information and statistics on the modern-day crisis of slavery, see www.globalslaveryindex.org.

2. Psalm 139:14.

3. Luke 11:1.

4. John 5:19.

5. Matthew 6:9.

6. See Exodus 13:21.

7. Matthew 5:17.

8. 1 John 4:8.

9. Genesis 3:1.

10. Genesis 2:16–17.

11. Quoted in Brennan Manning, *The Ragamuffin Gospel* (1990; repr., Colorado Springs: Multnomah, 2005), 25.

12. Reynolds Price, *Clear Pictures: First Loves, First Guides* (New York: Scribner, 1998) 74.

13. Psalm 34:3 ESV.

14. Matthew 7:11.

15. See Genesis 2:25.

16. Brennan Manning, *Abba's Child: The Cry of the Heart for Intimate Belonging* (1994; repr., Colorado Springs: NavPress, 2015), 39.

17. Revelation 4:8.

18. Acts 16:25.

19. David G. Benner, *The Gift of Being Yourself: The Sacred Call to Self-Discovery* (2004; repr., Downers Grove, IL: InterVarsity, 2015), 41.

20. Acts 16:26.

21. Matthew 6:10.

Chapter 4: Search Me and Know Me

1. Psalm 24:1–2.

2. Psalm 24:7–8.

3. Psalm 24:3–4.

4. Gilbert K. Chesterton, *Orthodoxy* (New York: John Lane, 1908), 24.

5. G. K. Chesterton, letter to the editor of the *Daily News*, August 16, 1905. See Jordan M. Poss, "What's Wrong, Chesterton?," *Jordan M. Poss* (blog), February 28, 2019, www.jordanmposs.com/blog/2019/2/27/whats-wrong-chesterton.

6. See Genesis 2:25.

7. I offer a fuller theology of this same definition in my previous book,

Searching for Enough: The High-Wire Walk between Doubt and Faith (Grand Rapids: Zondervan, 2021).

8. Genesis 3:9.

9. See Gary A. Anderson, *The Genesis of Perfection: Adam and Eve in Jewish and Christian Imagination* (Louisville, KY: Westminster John Knox, 2001), 135–54.

10. Genesis 3:11.

11. Eugene H. Peterson, *Christ Plays in Ten Thousand Places: A Conversation in Spiritual Theology* (Grand Rapids: Eerdmans, 2005), 316.

12. Psalm 51:4.

13. Genesis 3:24.

14. Psalm 24:4.

15. John 8:11.

16. Hebrews 4:15.

17. Hebrews 4:15.

18. Dane Ortlund, *Gentle and Lowly: The Heart of Christ for Sinners and Sufferers* (Wheaton, IL: Crossway, 2020), 50.

19. Mary Karr, *Lit: A Memoir* (New York: HarperCollins, 2009), 239.

20. Karr, *Lit*, 276.

21. Eugene H. Peterson, *Tell It Slant: A Conversation on the Language of Jesus in His Stories and Prayers* (Grand Rapids: Eerdmans, 2008), 186.

22. Psalm 139:1.

23. See "Story of the Moravians," Light of the World Prayer Center, https://lowpc.org/story-of-the-moravians; see also Pete Greig and Dave Roberts, *Red Moon Rising: Rediscover the Power of Prayer* (Colorado Springs: Cook, 2015), 75.

24. Brennan Manning, *Ruthless Trust: The Ragamuffin's Path to God* (San Francisco: HarperSanFrancisco, 2000), 48.

25. Isaiah 53:5.

26. C. S. Lewis, *The Voyage of the Dawn Treader* (1952; repr., New York: HarperCollins, 1994), 108–9.

27. This idea comes from Eugene H. Peterson, *Leap Over a Wall: Earthy Spirituality for Everyday Christians* (San Francisco: HarperOne, 1997), 189–90.

28. See 1 John 1:5–10.

Chapter 5: On Earth as It Is in Heaven

1. Walter Wink, *Engaging the Powers* (1992; repr., Minneapolis: Fortress, 2017), 322.

2. C. S. Lewis, *God in the Dock* (1970; repr., Grand Rapids: Eerdmans, 1998), 104.

3. Luke 11:1.

4. Matthew 6:9.

5. Matthew 6:9.

6. Matthew 6:10.

7. See Walter A. Elwell, ed., "Entry for Intercession," *Baker's Evangelical Dictionary of Biblical Theology* (Grand Rapids: Baker, 1997).

8. Richard Foster, *Prayer: Finding the Heart's True Home* (New York: HarperCollins, 1992), 191.

9. Rabbi Lord Jonathan Sacks, "The Love That Brings New Life into the World: Rabbi Sacks on the Institution of Marriage" (keynote speech, Colloquium on the Complementarity of Man and Woman, the Vatican and the Congregation for the Doctrine of the Faith, Vatican City, November 17, 2014), https://rabbisacks.org/love-brings -new-life-world-rabbi-sacks-institution-marriage.

10. Psalm 115:16.

11. See 1 Corinthians 12:27.

12. Isaiah 9:6.

13. John 12:31 ESV.

14. Matthew 28:18, emphasis mine.

15. John 16:7.

16. Alan Jones, *Soul Making: The Desert Way of Spirituality* (New York: Harper & Row, 1985), 167.

17. John 16:23–24.

18. Philip Yancey, *Prayer: Does It Make Any Difference?* (Grand Rapids: Zondervan, 2006), 143.

19. Larry W. Hurtado, *At the Origins of Christian Worship: The Context and Character of Earliest Christian Devotion* (Grand Rapids: Eerdmans, 1999), 107.

20. Quoted in Yancey, *Prayer*, 118.

21. P. T. Forsyth, *The Soul of Prayer* (1916; repr., Vancouver, BC: Regent College Publishing, 2002), 12.

22. John 16:24.

23. Pete Greig and Dave Roberts, *Red Moon Rising: Rediscover the Power of Prayer* (Colorado Springs: Cook, 2015), 88.

24. Eugene H. Peterson, *Tell It Slant: A Conversation on the Language of Jesus in His Stories and Prayers* (Grand Rapids: Eerdmans, 2008), 181.

25. Peterson, *Tell It Slant*, 182.

26. Visit the website of 24-7 at 24-7prayer.org.

Chapter 6: Daily Bread

1. Luke 3:11.

2. See "World Hunger: Key Facts and Statistics 2022," Action against Hunger, www.actionagainsthunger.org/world-hunger-facts-statistics.

3. Matthew 6:9–13.

4. This idea is explored in depth in Pete Greig's marvelous book *How to Pray: A Simple Guide for Normal People* (Colorado Springs: NavPress, 2019).

5. See Gustavo Gutiérrez, *We Drink from Our Own Wells: The Spiritual Journey of a People* (1984; repr., Maryknoll, NY: Orbis, 2003).

6. Ronald Rolheiser, *The Holy Longing: The Search for a Christian Spirituality* (New York: Doubleday, 1999), 66–67.

7. Julian of Norwich, *Enfolded in Love: Daily Readings with Julian of Norwich*, ed. Robert Llewelyn (London: Darton, Longman & Todd, 1980), 10.

8. See Luke 11:2–4.

9. John 5:6.

10. See Matthew 6:8.

11. See John 2:1–10; Mark 5:21–43; 10:46–52.

12. Charles H. Spurgeon, "Ask and Have: No. 1682" (sermon, Metropolitan Tabernacle, Newington, London, October 1, 1882), www.spurgeongems.org/sermon/chs1682.pdf, italics in original.

13. Richard Foster, *Prayer: Finding the Heart's True Home* (New York: HarperCollins, 1992), 50–51.

14. Exodus 32:14.

15. This idea was explored by John Mark Comer in *God Has a Name* (Grand Rapids: Zondervan, 2017), 61–62.

16. Malachi 3:6.

17. Hosea 11:8.
18. Comer, *God Has a Name*, 62.
19. Matthew 11:11, my paraphrase.
20. Dallas Willard, *The Divine Conspiracy: Rediscovering Our Hidden Life in God* (San Francisco: HarperSanFrancisco, 1998), 244.
21. James 4:2.
22. Matthew 7:9–11.

Chapter 7: The Middle Voice

1. Eugene H. Peterson, *The Contemplative Pastor: Returning to the Art of Spiritual Direction* (Grand Rapids: Eerdmans, 1993), 105.
2. Peterson, *Contemplative Pastor*, 104.
3. John 17:20–21.
4. John 17:22–23.
5. Genesis 3:12.
6. Luke 1:38.
7. Luke 1:48.
8. Psalm 112:6–7.
9. Luke 22:42.
10. Hans Urs von Balthasar, *Prayer*, trans. Graham Harrison (San Francisco: Ignatius, 1986), 14.
11. "Mother Teresa" (lecture, Norwegian Nobel Committee, Oslo, Norway, December 11, 1979). See "Mother Teresa Nobel Lecture," NobelPrize.org, www.nobelprize.org/nobel_prizes/peace/laureates/1979/teresa-lecture.html.
12. John 15:8.
13. Luke 11:39.
14. Luke 11:41.
15. N. T. Wright, *The Challenge of Easter* (Downers Grove, IL: InterVarsity, 2009), 53.
16. Luke 1:38.

Chapter 8: Laboring in Prayer

1. Cited in Pete Greig, *How to Pray: A Simple Guide for Normal People* (Colorado Springs: NavPress, 2019), 89.
2. See 1 Kings 18:20–24.
3. 1 Kings 18:30.

4. 1 Kings 18:33.
5. 2 Samuel 24:24.
6. 1 Kings 18:37–39.
7. See Exodus 20:5; 34:14.
8. Abraham Kuyper (speech, Vrije Universiteit, Amsterdam, Netherlands, October 20, 1880); quoted in James Bratt, ed., *Abraham Kuyper: A Centennial Reader* (Grand Rapids: Eerdmans, 1998), 461.
9. 1 Kings 18:38.
10. James 5:17 ESV.
11. Genesis 1:2.
12. See C. F. Keil and F. Delitzsch, *Commentary on the Old Testament*, vol. 1 (1861; repr., Grand Rapids: Eerdmans, 1991), 48.
13. Luke 1:35.
14. John 16:21.
15. John 7:38–39.
16. See the NASB New Testament Greek Lexicon, based on Thayer's and Smith's Bible Dictionary, public domain. Available online at "Koilia," Bible Study Tools, www.biblestudytools.com/lexicons/greek/nas/koilia.html.
17. Luke 9:54–56.
18. James 5:16–18.
19. Quoted in Pete Greig and Dave Roberts, *Red Moon Rising: Rediscover the Power of Prayer* (Colorado Springs: Cook, 2015), 190.
20. Cited in Greig and Roberts, *Red Moon Rising*, 269.
21. The story is told in Lewis A. Drummond, *Spurgeon: Prince of Preachers* (Grand Rapids: Kregel, 1992), 325.
22. Drummond, *Spurgeon*, 326; see also *Lutheran Herald* 1, no. 10 (March 8, 1906): 229–30.

Chapter 9: Ask, Seek, Knock

1. Mark 14:36.
2. Mother Teresa, *A Gift for God: Prayers and Meditations* (San Francisco: HarperSanFrancisco, 1996), 75.
3. Matthew 7:7.
4. Luke 18:1–8.
5. English translations that read this way include the Amplified Bible, the Holman Christian Standard Bible, the Complete Jewish Bible,

the International Standard Version, the New Living Translation, and the Orthodox Jewish Bible.

6. Luke 18:1.

7. Luke 18:4–5.

8. Luke 18:6–8.

9. Eugene H. Peterson, *Tell It Slant: A Conversation on the Language of Jesus in His Stories and Prayers* (Grand Rapids: Eerdmans, 2008), 144.

10. Revelation 5:8.

11. Revelation 8:3–5.

12. Psalm 56:8 ESV.

13. See Psalm 56:8.

14. Luke 18:8.

15. See Isaiah 53.

16. Parker Palmer, *A Hidden Wholeness: The Journey toward an Undivided Life* (San Francisco: Jossey-Bass, 2004), 82–83.

17. C. S. Lewis, *The Screwtape Letters* (1942; repr., New York: HarperCollins, 2001), 40.

Chapter 10: Rebellious Fidelity

1. This story is found in John 8:1–11. Unless otherwise indicated, the quotes are my paraphrase.

2. John 8:11.

3. John 15:9.

4. See Revelation 19:6–9.

5. Johannes Hartl, *Heart Fire: Adventuring into a Life of Prayer* (Edinburgh: Muddy Pearl, 2018), 205.

6. Henri Nouwen, "Letting Go of All Things," *Sojourners*, May 1979, 6.

7. Luke 11:1.

8. Matthew 6:9–10.

9. Jonathan Sacks, ed., *The Authorised Daily Prayer Book of the United Hebrew Congregations of the Commonwealth*, 4th ed. (London: Collins, 2006), 37.

10. Adapted from Pete Greig, *How to Pray: A Simple Guide for Normal People* (Colorado Springs: NavPress, 2019), 78.

11. As paraphrased by Ronald Rolheiser in *Domestic Monastery* (Brewster, MA: Paraclete, 2019), 41. The same passage appears this way in Dietrich Bonhoeffer's *Letters and Papers from Prison*: "As you

gave the ring to one another and have now received it a second time from the hand of the pastor, so love comes from you, but marriage from above, from God . . . It is not your love that sustains the marriage, but from now on, the marriage that sustains the love" ("A Wedding Sermon from a Prison Cell: May 1943," in *Letters and Papers from Prison* [1953; repr., London: SCM, 2001], 27–28).

12. David Brooks, *The Second Mountain: The Quest for a Moral Life* (New York: Random House, 2019), 139.

13. See Richard Rohr, "Contemplation and Compassion: The Second Gaze," in *Contemplation in Action* (New York: Crossroad, 2006), 15–16.

14. Psalm 55:16–17.

15. For more scholarly backing and biblical context, see Scot McKnight, *Praying with the Church: Following Jesus Daily, Hourly, Today* (Brewster, MA: Paraclete, 2006).

16. McKnight, *Praying with the Church*, 31.

17. See McKnight, *Praying with the Church*, 35.

18. See Matthew 5:13.

19. Acts 2:42.

20. See Paul Kroll, "Studies in the Book of Acts: Acts 2:42–47," Grace Communion International, https://learn.gcs.edu/mod/book/view.php?id=4475&chapterid=56.

21. Acts 2:43–47.

22. 1 Thessalonians 5:17 KJV.

23. See Genesis 26:18.

24. David Benner, *Desiring God's Will: Aligning Our Hearts with the Heart of God* (Downers Grove, IL: InterVarsity, 2015), 29.

25. Brooks, *Second Mountain*, 56.

26. See Matthew 11:28–30.

27. Matthew 6:10–11.

28. See McKnight, *Praying with the Church*, 31–32.

29. Eugene H. Peterson, *Tell It Slant: A Conversation on the Language of Jesus in His Stories and Prayers* (Grand Rapids: Eerdmans, 2008), 265, italics in original.

30. Matthew 26:42.

31. Matthew 6:9–10.

32. See John Michael Talbot, *The Jesus Prayer: A Cry for Mercy, A Path of Renewal* (Downers Grove, IL: InterVarsity, 2013), 52.

33. This famous saying of Zinzendorf is documented in many places, including Greig, *How to Pray*, 111.

34. John 8:11.

35. Mark 1:35.

36. John Mark Comer, *The Ruthless Elimination of Hurry* (Colorado Springs: WaterBrook, 2019), 82.

37. See McKnight, *Praying with the Church*, 61–65.

38. Luke 15:7.

39. Morris West, *A View from the Ridge: The Testimony of a Twentieth-Century Christian* (San Francisco: HarperSanFrancisco, 1996), 2.

40. "Dayenu: It Would Have Been Enough," My Jewish Learning, www.myjewishlearning.com/article/dayenu-it-would-have-been -enough.

Epilogue

1. Psalm 24:7.

2. Psalm 24:8.

3. Psalm 24:9–10.

4. 2 Samuel 6:17 KJV.

5. See 1 Chronicles 25.

6. David Fritch, *Enthroned: Bringing God's Kingdom to Earth through Unceasing Worship and Prayer* (Orlando, FL: Burning Ones, 2017), 25.

7. See Amos 9:11.

Appendix 1: The Intercession of Christ

1. Luke 2:14.

2. Isaiah 9:6.

3. Luke 4:21.

4. Mark 11:9–10.

5. John 19:30.

6. Matthew 27:46.

7. See Richard Bauckham, *Jesus and the God of Israel: God Crucified and Other Studies on the New Testament's Christology of Divine Identity* (Grand Rapids: Eerdmans, 2008), 255–56.

8. Acts 25:24; Romans 8:27, 34; 11:2; Hebrews 7:25.

9. Romans 8:33–34.

10. Romans 5:1, emphasis added.

11. Colossians 3:4, emphasis added.

12. Hebrews 7:25, emphasis added.

13. See Hannah Keyser, "Why Does 'K' Stand for 'Strikeout' in Baseball?," Mental Floss, October 25, 2016, www.mentalfloss.com /article/70019/why-does-k-stand-strikeout-baseball.

14. Dane Ortlund, *Gentle and Lowly: The Heart of Christ for Sinners and Sufferers* (Wheaton, IL: Crossway, 2020), 83, 85.

15. See Ortlund, *Gentle and Lowly*, 82.

16. Brennan Manning, *Abba's Child: The Cry of the Heart for Intimate Belonging* (1994; repr., Colorado Springs: NavPress, 2015), 9.

17. Genesis 4:1 ESV.

18. Frederick Buechner, *Secrets in the Dark: A Life in Sermons* (San Francisco: HarperSanFrancisco, 2006), 18–19.

19. See Genesis 2:25.

20. Kallistos Ware, "The Eastern Tradition from the Tenth to the Twentieth Century," in *The Study of Spirituality*, ed. Cheslyn Jones, Geoffrey Wainwright, and Edward Yarnold (New York: Oxford University Press, 1986), 254.

Searching for Enough

The High-Wire Walk between Doubt and Faith

Tyler Staton

A unique and validating look at the tension between disillusionment and a desire for truth, *Searching for Enough* helps you see your doubt not as an emotion to fear but as an invitation to be followed.

Do you ever find yourself thinking, *I'm not enough, and I'm never going to be. And I know I'm not supposed to say this, but God's not enough for me either.* Whether or not we attend church, deep down we wonder if the biblical story of faith is really enough for the complexity of the world in which we live. We fill our lives with other things, hoping that maybe the next experience or accomplishment will complete us. Yet with every goal we reach, we still feel discouraged and anxious.

In *Searching for Enough*, Pastor Tyler Staton draws on ancient and modern insights to introduce us, as if for the first time, to Jesus' disciple Thomas—history's most notorious skeptic. Like Thomas, we are caught between two unsatisfying stories. We want to believe in God but can't reconcile his presence with our circumstances and internal struggles.

But what if there's a better story than shame? What if there's a redemption so complete that there's nothing left to hide? What if there is a God who can heal your resentments, fears, and loneliness in such a profound way that you feel whole?

From a place of spiritual companionship and deep authenticity, Staton shows us it is not an empty tomb that will change our lives, but the presence of the living God. Whether you are a distant skeptic, an involved doubter, or a busy but bored Christian, *Searching for Enough* invites you to find enough in a God who offers the only promises that never disappoint.

Available in stores and online!